James Freeman Clarke

Modern Unitarianism

Essays and sermons

James Freeman Clarke
Modern Unitarianism
Essays and sermons

ISBN/EAN: 9783337159931

Printed in Europe, USA, Canada, Australia, Japan

Cover: Foto ©Lupo / pixelio.de

More available books at **www.hansebooks.com**

MODERN UNITARIANISM

ESSAYS AND SERMONS

BY

Rev. JAMES FREEMAN CLARKE, D.D., Rev. JOSEPH HENRY ALLEN, Rev. SAMUEL R. CALTHROP, Rev. BROOKE HERFORD, Rev. JOHN WHITE CHADWICK, Rev. MINOT J. SAVAGE, Rev. EDWARD EVERETT HALE, D.D., Rev. THOMAS R. SLICER, Rev. HOWARD N. BROWN, Rev. ANDREW P. PEABODY, D.D., Rev. ROBERT COLLYER, Rev. JOSEPH MAY

PHILADELPHIA
J. B. LIPPINCOTT COMPANY
1886

Copyright, 1886, by J. B. LIPPINCOTT COMPANY.

PREFATORY NOTE

The Essays and Sermons contained in this volume were delivered in connection with the dedication and opening of the new church-edifice of the First Unitarian Society of Philadelphia, in February, 1886, and a few references to the occasion of their composition are allowed to remain unchanged.

CONTENTS

	PAGE
DEDICATION SERMON. REV. JAMES FREEMAN CLARKE, D.D., OF BOSTON	7
A CENTURY OF UNITARIANISM IN AMERICA. REV. JOSEPH HENRY ALLEN, OF CAMBRIDGE	26
ISRAEL'S INSPIRATION AND OUR RELATION TO IT. REV. SAMUEL R. CALTHROP, OF SYRACUSE, NEW YORK	46
CHRISTIANITY IN THE PRESENCE OF MODERN CRITICISM. REV. BROOKE HERFORD, OF BOSTON	57
THE ETERNAL GOODNESS. REV. JOHN WHITE CHADWICK, OF BROOKLYN	72
THE DEBT OF RELIGION TO SCIENCE. REV. MINOT J. SAVAGE, OF BOSTON	93
THE CHURCH IN ITS RELATION TO PUBLIC CHARITY. REV. EDWARD E. HALE, D.D., OF BOSTON	116
THE CHURCH AS A SCHOOL OF ETHICS. REV. THOMAS R. SLICER, OF PROVIDENCE	130
RELIGION AND DEMOCRACY. REV. HOWARD N. BROWN, OF BROOKLINE, MASSACHUSETTS	150
THE SIMPLICITY OF THE GOSPEL. REV. ANDREW P. PEABODY, D.D., OF CAMBRIDGE	168
VISIONS AND PATTERNS. REV. ROBERT COLLYER, OF NEW YORK	183
A LIBERAL CHRISTIAN CHURCH. REV. JOSEPH MAY, OF PHILADELPHIA	198

DEDICATION SERMON

BY REV. JAMES FREEMAN CLARKE, D.D.

OF BOSTON, MASSACHUSETTS

"This I confess unto thee, that after the way which they call heresy, so worship I the God of my fathers."—ACTS xxiv. 14.

WE have assembled to-night to dedicate this building as a house of worship, a home for Christian work, a school of Christian education. It is a Unitarian Church which meets here for the worship of one God, the Father. It is a Christian Church, which takes Jesus of Nazareth as the leader of the human race in its ascent toward God, and in its brotherhood of love. This is not the first time that a Unitarian Church has been dedicated in Philadelphia. February 14, 1813, seventy-three years ago, the first Unitarian Church in this city was opened for the worship of the one true and living God. The society having outgrown the original building, a second was erected, and dedicated November 5, 1828. And now we meet to offer a third building to the service of God and man. But the Unitarian Church existed here long before its first house of worship was erected. In 1796 fourteen persons united for Unitarian worship in one of the rooms belonging to the University of Pennsylvania. For some years they were a church without a clergyman, and their services were conducted by the brethren. Three laymen—John Vaughan, Ralph Eddowes, and James Taylor—officiated as leaders of the worship of the society during several years, until about the time when William Henry Furness was ordained pastor in 1825, sixty years ago.

What has Unitarianism done during these years? What has it failed to do? What may it hope to accomplish in the future? Has it done its work, or is it only beginning to do it? And what do we, as Unitarians, owe to our faith? Such will be the subject of my remarks this evening.

In order to answer these questions it is necessary to consider the different methods by which truth extends and propagates itself. These methods take two principal forms,—outward and inward. Truth extends itself outwardly by teaching, discussion, controversy,— by associations, churches, constitutions, laws, and creeds. It also extends itself by an inward process, more silent, but not less powerful. By the constant influence of character it breaks down prejudices; by persistent loyalty to conviction it modifies belief; by the subtile, pervasive power of public opinion it disintegrates dogma and integrates new methods of thought. Christianity has acted on mankind in both ways. It built itself up as a community; it founded churches; it organized itself as an outward religion, with its creeds, its forms of worship, its sacraments, ministry, bishops, popes, monastic orders, solemn and noble architecture, majestic liturgies, institutions of charity and benevolence, missions. In this sense, and in this method of work, Jesus compared it to a seed. The resemblance is striking. As you cut open an orange or an apple, a seed drops into your hand. You look at it. It is a little thing, in its hard integument. Lay it away, and it may remain for years sleeping and unchanged. Put it in the ground, under favorable influences, and it awakes from its sleep. It thrusts down its tender roots, pushes up its soft stalk, grows, puts out leaves and branches, and at last becomes a tree. But there is nothing accidental in this development. What the tree shall be is foreordained from the foundation of the world. The tree with its special characters is potentially in the seed. Each seed must produce results after its kind.

So Christianity was once only a seed, a truth hidden in the soul of Jesus. But it grew up into that mighty tree we call Christianity, the leaves of which are for the healing of the nations. A tree may be beaten by storms, bruised and shattered in some of its limbs, its fruit may be injured by insects, men may graft alien branches into it, but the original life permeates the tree as long as it lives. So Christianity has had alien elements grafted into it from other religions; it has been wounded and bruised by bigotry, persecution, fanaticism; but it has been a shadow from the heat, a refuge from the storm, to multitudes of human beings; the birds of the air, homeless and restless spirits, have built nests in its branches; it has fed eager minds, comforted sad hearts in every age, and has been through all time a gospel of peace to mankind.

All Christian denominations are branches in this tree. It is divided into three vast limbs,—the Roman Catholic, Protestant, and Greek Churches. The Protestant limb has been subdivided into many branches,—Lutheran,

Calvinist, Episcopal, Baptist, Methodist, and the like. Each of these, like the tree itself, has grown out of an idea—a truth. Methodism was once a conviction, hidden in the soul of Wesley; Calvinism, a belief in the mind of Calvin. Each grows after its kind, bears fruit after its kind; but the life of the tree, Christianity itself, pours through them all.

Unitarianism is a small branch in this great tree. As a branch, as a visible church, it has grown very slowly. After an existence of nearly a century it has only some few hundred churches in this country, a few hundred in England, and a few hundred on the European continent. It has thus far failed of becoming a great denomination. The Methodist denomination, beginning about the same time, has its thousands of churches where we have our hundreds. We have not succeeded in forming a large organization, in building ourselves up into a great body. Why is this?

One reason of our failure in becoming a large denomination is to be found, I think, in the history of our origin. We began, as a protest against certain dogmas: the Trinity, the Deity of Christ, the Calvinistic doctrines of Hereditary Sin, Total Depravity, Atonement, and Everlasting Punishment. We opposed these doctrines on grounds of reason and Scripture, as not in accordance with the Gospel or the spirit of Christ. Our protest was enforced by appeals to the understanding, by arguments addressed to the logical faculty. But the understanding holds but a small place in the human brain. Its influence to move men to act is not powerful. Men do great things, not because logic makes it seem reasonable, but because the conscience commands;

the heart and the flesh cry out; the world of feeling, imagination, fear, and hope are stirred. A religion founded on appeals to the reason is not likely to build up a large denomination.

We were early charged with preaching a system of negations. As regards the general teaching of our pulpits this was far from being true. No men ever taught more earnestly the great positive truths of Christianity, God, Duty, Immortality, than the early Unitarians. Witness the writings of Buckminster, Channing, Ware. No men have advocated more zealously all humanities, charities, philanthropies, reforms. Witness the labors of Dr. Howe for the blind, of Dorothea Dix for the insane and the prisoners, of Dr. Tuckerman for the unchurched poor, of Horace Mann in the cause of education, of Charles Barnard for the children's church, of John Pierpont for temperance, and the antislavery efforts of Channing, Theodore Parker, Samuel J. May, Charles Sumner, John P. Hale, John Quincy Adams, John A. Andrew, and your former well-beloved pastor,— all of them earnest Unitarians.

Of the moral influence of the elder Unitarian preachers let me cite a single example. I knew, years ago, a wise and good man, Judge Speed, of Kentucky. He was a farmer and a slaveholder, but opposed to slavery, and ready to emancipate his slaves when he could see his way clear to do so. He gave freedom to those who were prepared for it, and was one of the most upright and benevolent of men. In his youth, when he was about to come of age, his father told him he ought to see something of the world, and allowed him to load a flat-boat with hemp and bacon and take it down to

New Orleans, and, having sold it, go round by a vessel to Philadelphia and come home on horseback over the mountains,—for such was the mode of travel in those days. He landed in this city on Sunday morning. He was just twenty-one. He was lonely in a strange place. Going through the street he passed near a church and went in. A venerable man, with flowing white hair, was preaching on the responsibilities and duties of life. He urged young persons, who were at the parting of the ways, to choose a true and noble purpose in life, to resolve to be good and useful men and women. The young man's heart was in a tender state,—he received the good seed into good ground,—and this was the turning-point in his life, as he told me many years afterwards. The preacher was Dr. Joseph Priestley. I cannot say in what pulpit he stood, for the Unitarian house was not then built.* But that sermon bore rich fruits. Abraham Lincoln was a friend and visitor in that family. A son of Judge Speed was a member of his Cabinet, and the influence of Dr. Priestley's sermon in Philadelphia, in 1797, working through Judge Speed on Abraham Lincoln, may have had an influence in helping the triumph of the right in the great struggle for Freedom and Union.

But, though so much positive work has been done by Unitarians in the cause of a broad religion and human progress, we admit that our technical theological work was largely negative, and could not but be so. Our

---

* Probably in the Universalist meeting-house. I have a letter in my possession, written from Philadelphia, February 14, 1796, by Hon. George Thatcher, of Massachusetts, in which he describes having just listened to a sermon given by Dr. Priestley in the Universalist meeting-house.

fathers were obliged by constant argument to contend against popular doctrines which seemed to them, and still seem to us, injurious to the mind and heart. But, necessary as was this preparatory work, it was one of the causes which has kept us from becoming a large sect.

Christianity is not so much a system of doctrines as it is a River of Life. It pours through the ages, from its far-off origin amid the hills of Nazareth, a current of action, of feeling, of faith, of religious sentiment, of hope for a better day, of confidence in things unseen, of trust in the Divine Presence and love, of loyalty to Jesus as Saviour and Master. The reason why the Roman Catholic Church is the largest of the great divisions of Christianity is that it was able to keep its place in the main channel of Christian tradition. The Protestant bodies were thrown a little out of that channel, and though borne onward by the living stream, have felt its power less. Some Protestant sects, like our own, have been swept still farther out of the main current of inherited life. The Society of Friends is another example of this arrested development in what seemed at first to promise unimpeded growth. That movement in its origin was characterized by an unexampled spiritual force and insight. It taught the doctrine of a Divine light and life in every human soul,—of the duty of universal love and brotherhood,—it was marked by the boldest radicalism. It modified essentially, in accordance with its fundamental principle, every doctrine then held by the Church. It substituted the Holy Spirit for the Bible as the supreme rule of faith; rejected the priesthood, clergy, sacrament; refused to take oaths, to have anything to do with military service, denounced human slavery, took care of its poor. In short, its general principle was so productive that it anticipated most of the reforms of the present hour. Why, then, has it not built up a great denomination, like that of the Baptists, Presbyterians, Methodists? The only reason I can find is that it passed out of the main channel of Christian life, and so has gradually lost the propelling power of the central stream.

The same explanation may be given of the limited extent of the Swedenborgian denomination, and of every other body which has become isolated, and which thus ceases to partake of the full life of the body. If a body chooses to separate itself from Christian sympathies it is its own fault; but when it is excluded from those sympathies it is the fault of the excluders.

There is still another cause which I must briefly touch upon for our want of larger success as an outward organization. Our people have not been sufficiently taught what they owe to their own denomination. We complain of the proselyting spirit of other sects, but we have gone to the opposite extreme of an ultra-liberality. Many among us seem to think it creditable not to care for the spread of Unitarian views or Unitarian churches. I once went with my friend, William G. Eliot, of St. Louis, to a Unitarian gentleman in Boston to ask him to contribute to Unitarian missions in the West. The gentleman said that he "did not believe in sending our doctrines where they were not asked for. We ought to wait until people felt the need of them." Dr. Eliot modestly replied, that it was "perhaps fortunate for us that the Apostles took a different view of their duties." Unitarians think it liberal to give more freely to the institutions of other denominations than to those of their own. They send their children to be educated in the schools of other sects and then express astonishment at finding them converted to Trinitarianism. They leave their own church and take a pew in that of another denomination, because it is nearer, because they like the music, or the ritual, or the preacher, never asking themselves whether they owe anything to the church in which they were educated to a knowledge of God and Christ. Is nothing, then, due to truth? Nothing to sincerity? Nothing to our fathers who have labored and suffered to break the yoke of an iron creed? Nothing to our children, to bring them up in a faith which leaves the mind free and presents God to the heart as a father of infinite love? Shall we hold as a trifle such great questions as are at issue between rational and orthodox Christianity? Either what we believe of God, Christ, and man is a matter of importance, or it is not. If it is of no consequence, let us abandon our churches and return into the current of Christian life. But, if it is of consequence whether we believe or disbelieve the Godhead of Jesus, the threefold personality of God, the total depravity of man, the vicarious atonement, and everlasting punishment, let us be loyal to our Church; let us be true to our convictions, and not be guilty of the unpardonable levity of treating such grave questions as of no consequence compared with what may please our taste or gratify our social ambition.

We have seen what Unitarianism has failed to do. It has failed thus far to build up a great denomination,—it has failed to destroy the old creeds. Let us now look at what it has accomplished.

I spoke in the beginning of the two methods by which truth propagates itself,—one outward, by visible institutions and organizations; the second inward, by an invisible influence. The first Jesus compared to a tree growing out of a seed; the other he likened to leaven, which a woman took and hid in three measures of meal till the whole was leavened. While as an organization Unitarianism has made small progress, as an influence it has accomplished more than its founders could have dared to hope.

Mr. Lecky, in his history of Rationalism, has shown us how beliefs, once universal, have passed away, not because of attacks made on them, or arguments against them, but by a silent and insensible movement. Thus during many centuries the belief in witchcraft was universal,—no one doubted or questioned its reality. Once it was believed to be a duty to put heretics to death. These beliefs have slowly faded away until nowhere in Christendom to-day, either in Catholic or Protestant countries, can any one be hung or burned as a witch or heretic. You can put your finger on no act of the Church, on no special date, when these beliefs were formally abandoned. But the advancing tide of Christian thought has leavened slowly and insensibly the opinions of men, till such practices have disappeared; as the warm spring days disintegrate and melt the icy surface of the mountain lake, which a few weeks before was almost as solid as stone.

I think we have a right to say that Unitarianism has in this same silent way leavened the views of other denominations. What changes have taken place in the old beliefs during the last half-century!

Unitarians have leavened the ideas of the churches as regards creeds. They opposed them on three grounds, —as conditions of fellowship, tests of character, and obstacles to progress. Fifty years ago the creeds were open to these objections. The Andover Creed was prepared for the express purpose of excluding a large number of the churches of New England from the fellowship of the rest. They were regarded as tests of Christian character. The Athanasian Creed declares that those who do not accept its mysterious and metaphysical definition of the Divine Nature shall without doubt perish everlastingly. Who believes that to-day? The old creeds remain, like dilapidated ruins of ancient monasteries, venerable for their age, regarded as interesting historical documents, but not considered as having authority (except "for substance of doctrine") over the belief of the Church to-day. They are occasionally examined to see what was the belief of former times, as we go out in the morning to look at a self-registering thermometer in order to find how low the mercury went the night before.

Unitarians have leavened the ideas of the churches as regards the Trinity. This doctrine is still retained in the creeds, but how seldom do we hear prayers addressed to the Triune God! Jesus said, "When ye pray say 'Our Father,'" and the churches now accept their Master's teaching, and agree with the Unitarians in giving the dear name of "Abba, Father," to our God. Paul said, "To us there is one God, the Father,"—and the churches are beginning to accept that apostolic statement. You might attend many Trinitarian churches a year and hear nothing of the Trinity. The only exception is the

Episcopal Church, which is compelled by its liturgy to address its prayers every Sunday to a being whose name is not found in the New Testament. Its liturgy anchors it to an outgrown belief. But, as the Church of England has revised the Bible, it is possible that it may one day admit that its liturgy is also capable of improvement, and conform itself to its Master's directions and example in worshipping the Father as the only true God.

Unitarians have leavened the ideas of the Church in regard to the divine character of Jesus. Dr. Channing long ago taught that the divinest element in Jesus was his moral character,—and that to claim for him the omnipotence of the Almighty was doing him less honor than seeing in him the very image of the divine goodness, the revelation of the heavenly love. The human life of this great leader of the race has been for years the object of study and enthusiastic interest by your former pastor. He has conferred an inestimable benefit on the whole Church by making the holiness and grandeur of Jesus a reality to us. What painting by Raphael of the disfigured Master brings him so near to us as the portraits of Jesus by the pens of Channing, Furness, Martineau, and Thom? And now we find the Church forgetting its metaphysical definitions of the consubstantial nature and hypostatic union, learning to love Jesus for his tender humanity, his sense of human brotherhood, his superior elevation of soul.

Unitarians have leavened the ideas of the Church as to the work of Christ. Denying that his death could be necessary to placate God, or satisfy the divine justice, or that Jesus could be punished for the sins of others, and proving the mediæval doctrine of the atonement to be equally opposed to reason and revelation, they have emphasized the work of Jesus as a salvation from sin. His work is a present one, to bring us to God and enable us to see the Father; to help us to trust in the infinite compassion; to rise from the death of sin to the life of righteousness; to lead honest, pure, and generous lives. They have taught that heaven and hell are both here, and that we must go out of the hell of selfish and worldly lives into the heaven of purity and peace if we would be saved by Jesus. The churches have not nominally rejected the old doctrines,—they still talk of atonement and expiatory sacrifice. But the meaning has gone out of these phrases, and they dwell more every day on the moral influence of Christ as the real salvation. We are saved by character, and in no other way.

And thus, too, have Unitarians leavened the creeds of the churches in regard to the hereafter. Formerly it was believed that death came as the punishment for sin, and an awful event; that after it was the day of Wrath, —"*Dies iræ, dies illa!*" Then followed the separation of mankind into two divisions,—the saints saved by the blood of Jesus, who were to be together in heaven, and the lost souls, who were to be thrust down to suffer torments with the devils in an everlasting hell. This creed, the outcome of Paganism, is still nominally held by numerous churches. But a higher and nobler view of God is beginning to prevail. We see that as God sends death as well as life to all His creatures—both must be blessings. Death, when it comes, must be a blessing. God must be the same in all worlds. Here He sends sun and rain on the evil and good, pouring out His gifts on

all, and He must do the same there. There, as here, He
will send us thought, work, affection,—enough to know,
enough to do, enough to love. There, as here, He will
give us the beauties and glories of nature, the sight of
great truths, the education of labor, joy, sorrow, difficulty, high hope, generous enthusiasm. There, as here,
He will surround us with generous affection, with kindly
sympathy, with the love of kindred hearts. We know
in part and teach in part; but we are sure of this, that
God will disinherit no child whom He has created, and
that if we choose to disobey Him and prefer to go down
into evil, His love will follow us still. "If I make my bed
in hell, Thou art there." His mercy endures, not for
seventy or eighty years, but forever. These great convictions of the Eternal Goodness are entering men's
hearts to-day, so that they can say with Whittier,—

> "Who fathoms the eternal thought?
> Who talks of scheme and plan?
> The Lord is God! He needeth not
> The poor device of man.
>
> "The wrong that pains my soul below
> I cannot place above.
> I know not of His hate. I know
> His goodness and His love.
>
> "I know not what the future hath
> Of trouble and surprise,
> Assured alone that life and death
> His mercy underlies."

Unitarians have leavened the Church with their views
in regard to the Bible and its inspiration. The old view
that every sentence in the Bible was the word of God

made the Bible a master and man a slave. It exalted the letter above the spirit. Paul declared, "The letter killeth, the spirit giveth life." The old view was idolatry,—for idolatry means worship of anything outward and visible. The old view confounded right and wrong,—justifying or excusing murder, cruelty, falsehood, and treachery when committed by Jewish saints. It set the Bible against science, and resisted the progress of human thought. Because the Bible said, "Thou shalt not suffer a witch to live," thousands of poor old women have been burned alive. Because the Bible says, "The sun ariseth and the sun goeth down," the Church denied the Copernican theory, and put Galileo in prison for saying that the earth went round the sun. This theory confused the conscience, stifled the reason, and destroyed the picturesque beauty of the Bible itself. The Bible is a lovely landscape, with lofty mountains soaring snow-clad to the sky,—the vast line of ocean reaching to the horizon,—sunny meadows, sparkling streams, dark valleys. The theory of literal inspiration makes of it a dead level; makes no difference between the inspiration of Elijah and that of Jesus; gives to the bitter complaints of Job and the dark despair of Ecclesiastes the same authority as to the Sermon on the Mount. Unitarians have resisted this theory from the first and have taught the higher doctrine of a spiritual influx. They have shown how inspiration rises from its earliest forms in Genesis and the Pentateuch, through David and the prophets, till it reaches its fulness in the teachings of Jesus. The old view looked to Elijah and Samuel, Deborah and Solomon, as giving us God's very word; the new view looks to Jesus as the author and finisher of our faith. This makes the Bible infinitely more interesting, because human throughout; a revelation not only of God, but of man, filled with the throbbing heart of humanity. It is a vast panorama of human life, with its aspirations and struggles, its errors and failures, its longings and its love.

Finally, Unitarians have laid stress on character as the highest aim of life, the great work of the Gospel, the Alpha and Omega of true religion. Undeterred by the cry that they were teaching "mere morality," they have asserted that only those who hear Christ's commands and do them have built their house on the rock. Unitarians have maintained that the purpose of the Gospel is not to save the soul from a future hell, but to cause the kingdom of God to come here and His will to be done on earth as it is done in heaven. They have declared that we are not to prepare to die, but to prepare to live, for if we live aright we shall always be ready to die. Emphasizing liberty of thought, and rousing the human mind to look freely at the highest problems, Unitarianism has developed in its churches what latent genius and intellect was in them, and has given to the nation a long list of its best scholars, statesmen, historians, poets, and philanthropists. And now we see this view accepted everywhere more and more and goodness recognized as the purpose of Christ's work. Since we find the Universal Church advancing along the same lines of thought which were opened by the early Unitarians, is it claiming too much to say that they have contributed to leaven Christendom in these directions?

Has Unitarianism done its work? So we are sometimes told. But I cannot think its work done while it continues to offer a religious home to those who cannot accept the popular creeds and are too honest to profess what they cannot heartily receive. It has not done its work as long as there is a great unchurched multitude of thinking men and women who are dissatisfied with the old forms and do not yet know of any other. Abraham Lincoln said he would join a church when he found one that had for its creed love to God and love to man. I receive letters frequently from different parts of the country, from those who have heard something of our teachings and who are longing to know more. As yet the churches, though moving forward, have not reached a point where they can satisfy every inquiring soul. Stopford Brooke told me that when he was thinking of leaving the Church of England, Dean Stanley begged him to remain, saying, "We need you and men like you to help us broaden the Church of England till it can hold all sincere Christians." Stopford Brooke replied, "Do you think, Dean, that in your time or in mine it will be broad enough to make Martineau Archbishop of Canterbury?" "I am afraid not," said Stanley. "Then it will not be broad enough for me," answered Brooke.

Is it not desirable—is it not necessary—that there shall be at least one denomination openly professing faith in Jesus, not as God, but as man; worshipping God, not as a Triune Being, but as the one God and Father of all? One denomination which shall claim to read the Bible with the understanding, as well as the heart, refusing to accept as Scripture anything it finds there inconsistent with the spirit of Jesus? One denomination fully believing the great words of Paul, that Faith, Hope, and Love are the vital and central elements of all religion, and that the greatest of these is Love? Unitarians need not oppose other Christian bodies. We recognize in all churches the great current of Christian faith and action. We also would be members of this body,—branches in this vine,—fellow-workers with our brethren in the same cause and under the same Master. We honor the good in all denominations; we reverence the goodly fellowship of the prophets and the noble army of martyrs; we sing the hymns of the ages; we are fellow-citizens of the saints and of the whole household of God.

Brethren of the Unitarian Church,—a church sanctified to us all by so many pure memories and sacred associations,—we wish you joy of your entrance into this beautiful house. Be not afraid or ashamed to say that after the way men call heresy, so you worship the God of your fathers. Stand fast in the liberty wherewith Christ has made you free, and be not subject again to any yoke of bondage. When John Vaughan and James Taylor and Ralph Eddowes with their few friends founded this Church, it would have been easy for them to say, "What is the use? What good will it do? Is it not better to conform to the old faith? We are only making ourselves unpopular, unfashionable. The old churches have all the prestige, the authority of long tradition, the power of wealth and numbers." But God had given them the sight of His truth, and they felt themselves bound to assert it and stand by it. They considered themselves debtors to mankind, and they went forward, doing their duty and leaving the results to God. This is the way that truth conquers error; when it inspires noble hearts with an ardent enthusiasm.

Let this house, then, be dedicated to the service of God the Father; of Jesus Christ, His dear son and our dear brother; of the divine spirit which is shed abroad in every open heart. Let it be dedicated to truth, to honesty, to justice,—to a religion, not for Sunday only, but for the whole week,—a religion not for this place only, but for the street, the shop, the lawyer's office, the editor's chair. Long may this religion be taught here, and be the inspiration and comfort of many souls, who hunger and thirst after righteousness.

3*

A CENTURY OF UNITARIANISM IN AMERICA

BY REV. JOSEPH HENRY ALLEN

OF CAMBRIDGE, MASSACHUSETTS

WE meet here on what is very nearly the hundredth birthday of Unitarianism in America. For, on the 19th of June, 1785, not quite one hundred years and eight months ago, the corporation of King's Chapel, in Boston, by a very large majority, voted to strike out from its Episcopal order of service all that teaches or implies the doctrine of the Trinity, and thus put itself openly upon the Unitarian ground on which it stands to-day.

This step was taken gravely and deliberately, as became the action of an ancient, respectable, wealthy, and conservative body, which that Church was then, and continues to be now. The way to it was laid in a course of discussions as to the true interpretation of Scripture doctrine, conducted by James Freeman, who, for about two years, had been the acting minister of that Church, and who, about two years later, was formally installed as its pastor by act of the congregation, the affiliated churches refusing their assent or fellowship. This independent course was favored also by the patriotic temper of the Revolutionary struggle a few years before, when some of the old loyalist proprietors went into exile, and their places were filled by younger men. The changes in the prayer-book were adopted from those which had been formulated, more than half a century earlier, by that highly intellectual group of clergymen in the Church of England, best known to us by the name and fame of Samuel Clarke. The result was not a secession, not a germ or suspicion of a new sect; but that a strong and intelligent religious body used its congregational freedom, under Massachusetts law, to stand upon ground which most men then deemed heresy; and that (in the words of Dr. Freeman's successor, Greenwood) "the first Episcopal Church in New England became the first Unitarian Church in America."

But in private the Unitarian opinion was pretty widely held, both before and after this act, quite outside of church lines and definitions. To say nothing of the loosening of old beliefs that always comes with a revolution in the State,—take Benjamin Franklin for an example,—there was a good deal of serious thinking among educated laymen in that direction. Thus Jefferson, says his biographer Randall, is to be reckoned a Unitarian in his belief; and that this Unitarian tradition continued in his family for at least two generations later, I had pleasant testimony during my own ministry in Washington. His correspondence, too, with his old friend and political rival, John Adams, gives many a proof that theology had a place in the thought of men of the world, and was no mere professional affair of a clique of theologians. This unprofessional and independent character has been a marked feature in Unitarianism from the start. The Unitarian movement, as it came up afterwards, was the offshoot of a large live body of opinion, having its roots deep in the common intellectual soil; it was not a local conceit, not a New England provincialism, not a sectarian revolt, as its enemies and even its friends have sometimes thought.

One incident of this earlier time has a special interest here: I mean the exile of Dr. Priestley and his landing in Philadelphia in 1794. Joseph Priestley was a man then of sixty-two, honored among the first names of European science, yet always, with a quiet and steady courage, ready to defend that reason in religion and that freedom of opinion which he held most precious to mankind. He shared, too, the enthusiasm of his time for political as well as mental freedom, which brought on him bitter persecution as a revolutionist. He had been driven from his home in Birmingham by a mob that burned his house, destroyed his books and laboratory, and scattered the costly record of his experiments to the wind,—claiming the connivance of all British respectability, as cowardly then as it was insolent, intolerant, and cruel. But when he landed in Philadelphia, an exile, poor, and growing old, the opportunity was offered him at once, both here and in New York, of founding a Unitarian congregation; here, too, with a professorship besides, which would continue without break his favorite pursuit of chemistry, where he stood second in eminence to no man then living,—for Lavoisier was guillotined that very year, and Dalton's great work in England began just after Priestley's death. But, like Cowper, he chose the country before the town; and so he went to Northumberland, on the Susquehanna, where he spent his declining years in the way of life he chose before any other; scrupulously fulfilling his duties as citizen and neighbor, corresponding widely with eminent men of like pursuits, making himself with serene piety a preacher of the faith for which he had patiently endured tribulation; and Northumberland is visited to this day by here and there a pilgrim loyal to that faith, revering in him one of the first and purest of pioneers in America of that liberal gospel whose advance we celebrate to-day. Nay, this fair and noble structure in which we gather to-day is one ripened fruit out of the many that have grown directly from the seed planted then.

Some Unitarians of a later day have been at pains to disclaim Priestley's "materialism,"—perhaps without appreciating so well as he that mystery of matter, which made him see in it reverently, like Tyndall, "the potency and the promise of all forms of life." His multifarious industry, spread over wide departments of study in eight-and-twenty volumes, may look shallow and suspicious to the deeper learning and severer criticism of our time. He accepted, childlike, many an opinion taken from his literal rendering of the Bible, which has been dropped since, and left far behind. He put forth, with amazing simplicity, crude explanations of prophecy, which he would no more have accepted than we do, if he had lived through any five of the last fifty years. But his piety was as tender and reverent as if he had been bred up in all the aspirings of our new transcendental gospel. His religious trust was as serene as that of the most radiant modern optimist. For wise and faithful discipline of life, where shall we find a better pattern of the virtues we hold nearest allied to

a liberal faith? His theological enemies in England
echoed, perhaps prompted, the vilest execrations of the
Birmingham mob. Edmund Burke, with superfluous
disdain, refused to answer or even to notice an appeal
for justice in behalf of this ecclesiastical outlaw. At a
local gathering of clergy (we are told) one man said he
would gladly set the torch with his own hand to a pile
of Priestley's writings and burn the author alive with
them; and all the rest, applauding, declared themselves
ready to do the same. Such was the insolence of theo-
logic hate in England a hundred years ago! It is among
the honorable memories of this community, and of that
time, that a generous welcome was given to the exile
here, where the name heretic has never yet been held
good ground to repudiate all human charity.

This hospitable welcome Priestley enjoyed for about
ten years, till his death in 1804. One year later, the
growing liberal spirit in New England scored its first
conspicuous triumph, in the appointment of Henry
Ware, then a modest country minister at the age of
forty-one, a man of singularly blended sweetness of
temper, austere integrity of conscience, absolute intellectual candor, and a touching humility of spirit, as
Divinity Professor in Harvard College. The new theology had now found a home and a centre of influence in
our oldest and most potential seat of learning. And
these words meant more then than they might seem to
mean now. Harvard College had not only been in a
peculiar sense the care of the State since its foundation
within six years after the origin of the colony. It had
come to be identified, more closely than is usual with
American colleges, with the life of the community

about it; so that its history includes, in extraordinary proportion, the lives and work of men who gave tone to politics, arts, letters, society, and business in what we may call the metropolitan region of New England. Liberal theology was at once known to be a power, when thus adopted by that intellectual authority. In five years more, Dr. Kirkland, one of the most brilliant and eminent of the liberal preachers of the day, an intellect clear, wise, genial, vigorous, and serene, was made President of the University. A group of men, including such names as Joseph Stevens Buckminster, William Emerson, Edward Everett, Nathaniel Langdon Frothingham, and Samuel Thacher, among the Boston clergy, began soon to give shape and breadth to the movement, first through literary circles, then by such channels as the *Monthly Anthology*, the *North American Review*, and the series of journals that represented the several stages of theological advance. Of these the widest known and longest lived was the *Christian Examiner*, whose pages are the real history of that movement for forty-five years, till it ceased in 1869. It may be truly said that the best and most characteristic thought of the best and most characteristic writers who, for that long time, represented the movement is to be found in the files of that one journal.

But it was not until 1815—thirty years after the date I began with—that the name Unitarian seems to have been given to and accepted by the new school of thought. Accepted, I say, though reluctantly, and not by all. For some of its best-known leaders, as Channing and Norton, had a great distrust of any name that looked ever so remotely like the founding of a new sect.

Let it be Congregational, or Independent, or Liberal, or Independent Congregational,—any name but that. They wished it to be a free movement of thought, conscience, and life within the lines of the old Congregational order, which was theirs by birthright, and which they never wished to leave. But, without choice or desire of theirs, the movement soon carried them beyond those lines, and must be known by another name. And so, for seventy years, we have to consider Unitarianism in America as a body with a name and history of its own, its own traditions and its own organic life.

These seventy years, as we look back upon them now, fall easily into three pretty well marked periods, of something over twenty years each: one was the time of drawing denominational lines and settling into shape, —a process rudely interrupted by the breeze of transcendental speculation, about fifty years ago; one of much self-criticism and widening differences of opinion, roughened, too, by the passions and perils that merged at length in the great storm of our civil war; one of the more vigorous organization and wider enterprise that have followed since the war. I should like, in my brief review, to keep these three divisions as clearly in sight as possible.

The first is the period of the Unitarian controversy proper, and of what is sometimes called "old-school Unitarianism," which then came to its full growth and its completest social ascendency. The movement was almost wholly local, being mostly confined to the circle of Eastern Massachusetts, though represented in a few vigorous colonies extending as far south as Charleston, Savannah, and Mobile, and as far west as the Mississippi at St. Louis and New Orleans, Boston being, however, always looked to fondly as "the Jerusalem of our faith." There, indeed, it was almost completely identified with the best intelligence, the highest social rank and culture, the morality and humanity, the arts, learning and letters, the political eloquence, the professional and public life of the community, so that at one time it might almost be taken for granted that a man eminent there in any of those ways was in the Unitarian circle. Indeed, I can recall in history only the single case of Geneva under Calvin, where an independent religious movement has so thoroughly taken possession of a community, heart, mind, and soul, as this did fifty to sixty years ago, in what is now called "the metropolitan district" of Massachusetts. That was the period of "Boston Unitarianism," best, most widely, most lovingly, most honorably known to the world, then and now, by the revered name of William Ellery Channing. Its most permanent monument of that day is the American Unitarian Association, founded in 1825, which has been the agent of its widest activities and largest charities, and is such to this day.

The second period had its new enthusiasms, its greater heat of passion, its restless speculations and disturbed beliefs. Old confidences had to give way, new controversies and perils had to be anxiously met. The same temper that was eager to strike at the old foundations, was just as eager in its confidence that the new faith could never be disturbed; such names as agnostic and pessimist, so common now, had not yet been so much as named among us. And all this, with the incessant collision between the church life of piety and the aggressive conscience, hot to grapple with all shapes of private sin, or social wrong, or public guilt. This period is best known to us, and will always be best known, by the name of Theodore Parker. His life came to an end with the period I have described, at the very eve of the civil war he had long foretold. His true work in the field of religious thought has just received its full recognition—where it would have been most grateful to him—in the communion which, forty years ago, ventured neither to own nor to disown his fellowship. A handsome volume of his writings was published by the American Unitarian Association a month ago; and his portrait will have its place among those we delight to honor in the noble denominational building now near completion.

The period since the war has had the great good fortune of being inspired and led by that most loyal, trusted, and beloved of leaders, Henry Whitney Bellows, alike honored in his lifetime and gratefully held in our memory, that knows better with each year the value of the work he left behind. For to him we owe almost everything we have that gives form and vigor to our denominational life: our methods of organization, our vision of the wide field open to us now, and the still broader future. His life is our cherished example of generous enthusiasm, unflagging energy, unwearied labor, unstinted sympathy, unsparing self-devotion, for whatever good thing made appeal to that splendid capacity of work, that vigorous, manly conscience, that munificent and royal soul.

These three we may put in a rank by themselves, as specially or severally representing the three periods I have kept in view. But besides these a great and rich diversity of gifts has been included—not always, indeed, quite harmoniously—within our narrow denominational lines. Many other names deserve well to stand in even the briefest record that attempts to sum up our grateful recollections. There are those dear and honored veterans among the living—Furness, Hedge, and Eliot—whom we esteem very highly in love for their work's sake. Among our revered dead I recall the names of Orville Dewey, a man of unique power in the pulpit, which was his throne,—in whom thought was more intimately blended with emotion than in any other great preacher we have listened to or could easily name,— who seemed to make the sacred desk a confessional to whisper the most secret things of the religious life,— whose large and brooding intellect set itself to interpret the soul's deepest experience in the terms of freshest knowledge and youngest thought,—whose mind was generously open till long past eighty to the latest methods or discoveries in the pursuit of truth; George Putnam, whose clear, argumentative statement commanded the respect of the ablest lawyers, whose large sense matched the worldly wisdom of statesman and financier,—the eloquent orator of homely morality and the religion of every-day life, which his touch transfigured to poetry and splendor; President Walker, most grave and candid of divines, honored alike in clerical as in academic life,—whose shrewd wisdom, generous tolerance, wide philosophic culture, and dignity of character were not more marked than the cordial and kindly sympathy he always had for younger men; Samuel Gilman, whose clear, serene, and faithful spirit has stamped itself more deeply on the religious life of his own communion and been more completely reflected in the perfect and abiding loyalty of many disastrous years since he passed away, than is often given to be the reward of even such patient and consecrated services as his; Theodore Clapp, who with cheerful courage and unaltered buoyancy of religious hope stood at his post in New Orleans through many and many a pestilential month, and has left in his autobiography a most unique and charming record of a most extraordinary work; John Pierpont, tender religious poet and high-tempered pulpit combatant,—proud, irascible, always eagerly pressing home some sharp point of his generous and hot conviction; Samuel Joseph May, that brave saint of all the humanities, in whom sweetness and courage were more perfectly blended than in any other we have known,—whose great heart, by a generous instinct, went out every way to the poor, the forsaken, and the oppressed,—whose temper was so radiant with kindly humor that we who loved him may say that only to have looked upon him was a sort of sunshine in one nook, at least, of the most unfriended life; Ephraim Peabody, the well-beloved minister of King's Chapel, whose face was a benediction,—who so patiently endured much poverty and sorrow in his earlier ministry that its later prosperity and joy was always touched with that serene humility of spirit,—in whom gravity, sweetness, and a cautious wisdom were gathered in a combination as rare as it was pure and lovely; Ezra Stiles Gannett, most fervent and devoted of men—whose conscience, morbidly acute, was burdened with every grief and sin of the city where he did his noble work,—whose burning speech almost inspired the cool temper of Boston Unitarianism with his own missionary zeal,—of whom it may well be said that ten such men would have carried Unitarianism like a prairie-fire from shore to shore of our continent; Thomas Starr King, that bright electric light of liberal theology, whose flame went out, alas! on the Pacific coast, twenty-two years ago,—whose memory is wonderfully fresh and near to us who loved him, as the most genial of friends, the most cheerful and instructive of companions, the most lucid, swift, and radiant intelligence that it has ever been our joy to know.

But the Unitarian movement, from the beginning, has belonged quite as much to thoughtful and intelligent men of the world as to professional preachers or theologians. If I were to attempt a list of men eminent in politics, in letters, in professional or business life, on the bench or at the bar, or in the Senate, more or less closely associated with that movement,—from John Quincy Adams, most learned and best equipped of American statesmen, whose service to the public began ninety-five years ago, to Henry Kidder, a man of equal integrity, generosity, gentleness, wisdom, and business faculty, whom we lost only the other day; a list to include such names as Judge Cranch of Washington, Judge White of Salem, Judge Lyman of Northampton, Senator Sumner and Governor Andrew of Massachusetts, Theodore Sedgwick of New York, James Perkins of Cincinnati; the poets Bryant and Longfellow; Huidekoper of Meadville, Howard and Sprague of Buffalo, Crowe of St. Louis, Whitridge of Charleston, besides the large cluster of the most eminent New England names of that time, and the lesser groups elsewhere of noble pioneers of the liberal faith,—

you would see that not one of them stands for a merely theological opinion, or for service to a sect. They all stand for service to humanity, in the largest sense they could give to that grand phrase; for the life that goes forth from the true Church of Christ into the heart and conscience of a people, to inspire its better thought of justice, to serve its higher education, to guide and instruct its counsels, to direct its works of noblest charity, to feed and sustain its holiest affections, to sanctify and ennoble its better hopes. That has been the quality of the work they have done.

And that has been the significance of this movement in religious history. It has been not the creation of a sect, but the progressive liberalizing and widening out of a church life that had its roots far back in the soil of a history, and has never severed its connection with the past. Of a list of three hundred and sixty Unitarian churches, one hundred and twenty or more—that is, full one-third—were originally local parishes, founded under the first ecclesiastical polity of the Puritan colonists, and dating before the war of the Revolution. These have brought down to our day, and into contact with the foremost advance of modern thought, the original inheritance of that great Puritan stock, which founded the English Commonwealth of Cromwell and Milton, and sent forth from its bosom the Pilgrim Fathers of our American Republic.

And again, the motive of this movement has been no narrow sectarianism, no theological pedantry and conceit; but in the truest sense an *ethical* motive,—that is, one which sought a better faith and a purer righteousness. Its great manifesto, that which first gave it (so to speak) consciousness of itself and the courage of its convictions, was Channing's celebrated discourse in Baltimore, May 5, 1819. Look a moment at the argument of that discourse. Under its first head, it pleads for the use of Reason in the interpretation of the Bible. Under the second head, it deals with these five topics: 1, the unreason of the Trinity, especially the confusion of thought as to the true object of worship; 2, the like confusion induced by the metaphysics of Christ's twofold nature; 3, the moral paradox of the alleged conflict of justice and mercy in the Divine government; 4, the moral enormity of the doctrine of vicarious atonement; 5, the true nature of holiness as a condition of the soul, contrasted with the doctrine of arbitrary "imputation." The discourse is less a theological argument than a solemn impeachment of the orthodoxy of that day, at the bar of the popular reason and conscience; and the impeachment was so effectively made, that we may doubt whether a single reputable orthodox pulpit in America would maintain at this day the naked Calvinism which he assailed. Channing, it may be charged, was not a learned theologian, not a master in metaphysics, not erudite and profound in controversy. No believer in the Trinity that ever lived would, it may be, accept his statement of it; no student of the history of doctrine would infer that he understood its meaning or value in past ages as a symbol in religious thought. But no man ever put more cogently than he did the plain language of reason and conscience, as it goes out to the common mind; and against this, scholastic metaphysics, such as he attacked, proud and formidable as it might look, a terror as it might be to many a pious soul, is really as vain as the stormy foam that dashes furious but helpless against a rock.

In this brief review I must omit almost wholly the middle period of our denominational life,—that time of interior controversy and division, which began nearly fifty years ago, with the so-called "transcendental" movement, and continued till just before our civil war. That time was loud and incessant in pressing its claims upon our notice then, and it has had its full share in the attention we have given since to the study of our history, so that it the less requires to be dwelt on here. We are happy in having outgrown its mutual distrusts, and outlived its acrimonious debates. And if these did not, as many of us feared they would, entirely break up our bonds of mutual trust and loyalty, that was—as we may hope now—because a larger and better work lay before us, for which we needed all that training to prepare.

What I have left to say, then, is of the period that has passed since the war, and is passing now. That great shock woke us all to the sense of a broader field and a deeper ground of union for our work. Sectarian lines were wonderfully broken and blurred in the new passions, the new sympathies, of that dread struggle. At the end of it, we know that we had entered upon a new phase of national life; and that whatever is to tell upon that life must have a larger and more generous interpretation. Still, it hardly seems as if we should have quite realized our new opportunity, with its grander possibilities, but for our great good fortune, just then, in having one man, every way equipped to be our leader; one man who, with fervent and almost childlike loyalty to our earlier tradition, had a confidence in our future equally ardent and intense, sympathy the most generous with younger and perhaps less reverent minds, enthusiasm only equalled by his untiring capacity of work, and the personal qualities to enlist the devoted attachment of his followers. However clear the summons, however wide and inviting the field of opportunity, yet we should hardly have known what either of them meant if we had not had that one interpreter.

You will remember that on the very week when the great news began to come in, that told how the nation was at length past her dreary tragedy, victorious and safe, there was gathered in New York, by the counsel and under the inspiration of Dr. Bellows, the first of the series of National Conferences, which have proved—spite of some errors and misgivings—the chief directing and inspiring agency in our later plans of action. You may, perhaps, also call to mind the ardent confidence with which he urged that our form of faith would, more than any other, give the type of the American religion of the future; that its ripening, slowly and long prepared for, would come at length in a sudden consciousness, born in the national heart at large, of a broad, unsectarian, and rational conception of the Divine life, such as has always made the ideal of our religious thought. This might not take the name we have known it by, for Unitarianism is our opinion, not our faith. But, for himself, he was a champion of the Unitarian cause *as such;* he was always for rallying heartily about that banner, and doing heartily the denominational work. Only, that banner must represent nothing sectarian and mean. It must not signify, it must not even hint, a creed. Spiritual affinity and willingness to unite in the

common work must be the only test. All who chose to
rally round it were sure of his large-hearted welcome.
No lines of doctrine should be drawn to rule out any
honest and willing mind. His own opinion, however
devoutly held, was as little a test to him as any other
man's opinion. Whatever of candid and instructed
thought, of serious purpose, of devout emotion, of zeal
for the Lord's work, could join in to make part of the
larger life in the coming age of faith, all should be em-
braced in that Unitarianism which is "the unity of the
Spirit in the bond of peace."

Under such guidance as I have described, the Unitarianism of our day is far more explicit and vigorous in
its self-assertion than in the early years of its life.
Then, as we have seen, the very name was accepted
with reluctance and distrust; any corporate work was
undertaken with hesitation, often with astonishing irres-
olution and lack of practical skill; at every new division
of opinion, or theological secession, there was a pretty
wide apprehension that its day was wellnigh over, and
its best work done. Now, for the doing of that work,—
besides the munificence bestowed upon local objects,
such as the building of costly temples like this in which
we meet,—at least ten times the amount is expended
from year to year on its larger enterprises, extending
from India in the East to the waters of Puget Sound,
that was bestowed fifty years ago, when socially Unitarianism stood at its highest. A defined and formal
fellowship is recognized under that name, embracing
the Unitarian communities of Transylvania and those
in England, with a scattered few in France and Italy,
in one brotherhood. Now, the name is frankly and

even rather proudly avowed. It is put in conspicuous letters on a massive building, whose walls of hewn and unhewn stone might make "a mighty fortress" of our faith for a thousand years. It is adopted by a great and wealthy club, that might suffer reproach as aristocratic if it did not vigorously and intelligently deal with all high matters of ethical and social concern. It is chosen, instead of the more enticing term "liberal," to designate the religious life, at once serious, progressive, and free, that organizes itself in churches in the wide spaces of the growing West. It rallies, in our National Conference and elsewhere, that warm-hearted and open-handed loyalty, which gathers so much more readily about a cause that frankly puts forth its symbol and its name, and seems to have the courage of its convictions.

I have said before that one-third of our three hundred and sixty congregations belong to the old local churches of New England, and date their foundation before the Revolutionary war. Another third belong as distinctly to this latest period of our history, and date their existence since the close of our civil war. And these are so far from being bounded by the geographical limits which used to be our reproach, that they are found in twenty-four of the States, ranging from Maine and Georgia on the east to California and Oregon on the west. While our two chief organizations care for the interests of the Eastern and Valley States, we send this very month a missionary eager and full of faith to that region, of singular beauty, wealth, and promise, which lies along the fifteen hundred miles of our Pacific coast. The objects of our concerted effort have included, in these last years, extended educational or missionary effort throughout the South, a mission to India of the Orient, and active agencies in the wide spaces occupied by our Indians in the West. And these, our larger enterprises, show a variety, a zeal, a persistency, an intelligence of labor, a definiteness of aim, and often an organizing skill, a general agreement in purpose and spirit, spite of much difference in opinion and occasional lack of harmony, which, to us who have weathered the sharper acerbities of forty years ago, may well seem to teach only the needful lesson of patience and mutual trust.

Then, too, we have proved by experience the capacity of our lax and easy-fitting organization to take in without damage opinions that lay far beyond the horizon of religious thought visible or conceivable to our predecessors. The period of most anxious difference among us was ushered in by three prophetic voices uttered by Emerson in three successive years: "Nature," in 1836, "The American Scholar," in 1837, and the "Divinity School Address," in 1838. How impossible it then seemed to many, that these notes should be harmonized with the freest word of Christian faith, some of us well remember; but now, to as many, they speak the very central truth that makes us one. Ten years later, the first intelligible hints of the natural development of species in "Vestiges of Creation" caused a shiver, as if of a coming storm of unbelief; but now, to very many, the far more radical theories of Darwin and Spencer are in direct line with the religious thought they find most light and comfort in. None of these things now disturb, in the slightest degree, our sense of fellowship. The freedom we were born to, or else have won, will not be allowed, now we have got it, to cripple and sunder those who, after all, are united in one work.

For, as we may well believe, there is a definite contribution to be made, one which we in especial are commissioned to make, to the higher life of our American civilization. Rich, vigorous, prosperous, and strong that civilization doubtless is; but hard, proud, remorseless, and full of social peril, except it be tempered by the spirit which has been nurtured through so many Christian centuries. We shall not stand in the way of whatever any others, from Catholic to Comtist, may contribute; but, as we hold, God has given us also our own work to do. The lesson of that century of Unitarianism in America which we have now looked back upon, surely is, that that work we have to do at any rate; and that we need not, must not, fail of the courage, the harmony, and the hope, which are our pledge that we shall not have run in vain, neither labored in vain.

ISRAEL'S INSPIRATION AND OUR RELATION TO IT
BY REV. SAMUEL R. CALTHROP
OF SYRACUSE, NEW YORK

HUXLEY, in his life review the other day, declared that it was difficult to realize that, when he was a boy, the world had no better means of locomotion than Achilles had at the siege of Troy. When I think of the religious world into which I was born, the difference between that world and the world I live in to-day becomes almost incredible to the mind.

It was a narrow world. It was made six thousand years ago, and would probably be destroyed within another thousand. It had no vistas of immeasurable time, no outlook into immeasurable space. All was small, narrow, confined, stifling.

It was a gloomy world. The blackness of darkness, darkness hopeless, irremediable, covered it. The most appalling part of this darkness was that it was eternal. God himself had foreordained and foreseen its utter hopelessness; and it was the very refinement of blasphemy even to express the faint hope that, in some far, far future, the darkness might possibly be lifted. It was of no use for ardent, loving souls to labor. The sure word of prophecy had long ago gone forth, that only a small portion of mankind could ever be rescued. The doom had been pronounced beforehand.

It was a cowardly world. Since favor to the individual could only be obtained by acquiescence in the so-called divine will, he that would be saved could only be saved at the cost of his manhood. It was a world anxiously awaiting the swift-coming shipwreck, and eager to jump into the Captain's boat, leaving all the rest of the passengers and crew, men, women, and little children, to drown. It was a world whose house was on fire, and father and mother were eager to rush first to the fire-escape and leave the babes in the cradle to be burned up. It was a world where friend was ready to betray friend, the parent be false to his child, the husband to ignore the wife of his bosom. A man was ready to give his manhood in exchange for his soul!

It was all this and more and worse, in theory. The general outlook on the universe and on man's destiny within it was simply an atrocity. But all this time sweet human charities went on. Beautiful tenderness, gentleness, sweetness, made gracious a thousand homes. Tens of thousands whose theory was the Westminster Catechism lived the Sermon on the Mount. The story of the Cross still bore its appropriate fruit in lives consecrated wholly to the service of God and man. For, while the creed as to man's destiny in general was abominable, instructions to the individual in holy living were glorious and bore much fruit. Whence this amazing jumble of things good and things bad? This nightmare dream of fire and brimstone, mixed up in inextricable confusion with the light of heaven? Very largely it came from the fact that Europe's religion was exotic, not native to the soil. Europe had Europe's art, Europe's science, Europe's literature, Europe's philosophy, but she had adopted Israel's religion. Her culture was European, her worship was Asiatic. Europe had accepted Israel's results, accepted them pretty much all in a lump; accepted, without any sifting, every fragment that Israel had written, accepted the crudest first guesses of semi-barbaric Israel, and put them absolutely on a par with Israel's last and divinest word. Europe insisted that everything Israel had written was the infallible word of God. All was on a par. It was blasphemy to assert that there was the least difference between Samuel hewing Agag in pieces and ordering the slaughtering of every man, woman, and child of the Amalekites, and the "Love your enemies" of the gospel: between Elijah killing four hundred and fifty priests of Baal, and Jesus' "Father, forgive them."

Europe thus accepted what Israel herself had rejected —accepted what Israel had slowly and painfully outgrown and left behind. Israel's religion was worked out by Israel's own experience, and it was therefore organic, vitally connected with Israel. Europe accepted Israel's results ready made, and, therefore, these results could not be organically connected with Europe's experience. Hence the results which followed. Europe had already developed a glorious art, a many-sided literature, a keen philosophy, and had at least awakened science. Europe accepted the religion of a people who ignored art, despised philosophy, and had not made a single contribution to science. Had Europe developed a grand religious consciousness on her own line, her art would have been purified, not swept away: her science would have been developed, not ignored: her philosophy would have been stimulated, not silenced.

Now, what is our task to-day? It is to retrace the organic growth of Israel's religion, to restudy the record in the light of modern thought: to accept all that is of everlasting significance, putting aside the accidental, the partial, the outgrown. When we open the Hebrew Bible, Genesis, the book of "Beginnings," rightly comes first, not because it was written first—for though much of it is old, much was written quite late—but because it treats of primeval subjects. Within the last few years the dead and buried Assyrian literature has come to life again, and we find, to our surprise, that the first eleven chapters of Genesis have been largely derived from Assyrian or Babylonian sources. The original source is the great epic, which was written in the Accadian language, a branch of the Turanian, and was translated into the Assyrian, or Chaldee, language in the eighth century B.C. The most conservative scholars date this epic back to at least to 2000 years B.C. Of this many fragments have already been discovered. It consisted of twelve books, of which we now have the sixth entire, and a considerable part of the eleventh, with many portions of the rest. In it we find the ideas of the creation, the fall of man, the sacred tree, the guardian cherubs, and the flaming sword. The tower of Babel is there also, and the account of the deluge, which was the subject of the eleventh book, has been largely recovered. The hero of the deluge is warned by heaven of the approaching flood, and is ordered to build a ship, and put into it "his household and the fruits of the field." He "pitched the ship within and without with pitch." (See Gen. vi. 1, and forward.) Then the rain flood came, and "destroyed all life from the face of the earth." On the seventh day the ship rested on a mountain. After seven other days Tamzi, the Noah of the poem, sent forth a dove and a swallow, which both returned to the ark, and a raven, which returned no more. After this it is impossible to doubt that the Biblical accounts and this have a common origin. The so-called creation tablets discovered and translated by Mr. George Smith are still fragmentary, but their parallelism with Genesis i. cannot be doubted. Even Genesis x. must be admitted to be the result, mainly, not of Jewish, but Assyrian study in geography and ethnology.

What, then, is the most probable conclusion? A few may still endeavor to account for these phenomena by supposing a tradition common to the Hebrews and Accadians, preserved unbroken for two thousand years; in some parts preserved nearly word for word. But it is easy to predict that the final result will be the acknowledgment that the first eleven chapters of Genesis are mainly a transcription of Assyrian ideas by the Hebrews, with a noble infusion of the grander monotheism of the latter. But when did the Hebrews become so intimately acquainted with Assyrian literature? We can find no trace of such acquaintance in the earlier prophets, but Ezekiel, the prophet of the captivity, shows the influence of Babylonian thought on every page. Is it not, then, highly probable that we owe at least a large portion of these chapters to the captive scholars of Israel, who, at Babylon, had for the first time, in Babylonish libraries, the opportunity to come into direct contact with this grand literature? To them, then, in this case, the world owes it that the touching pitiful legend of Adam and his Eve, his paradise, his sin, his sorrow, and expulsion has come to be part of the world's thought. But now comes the question: If once the origin of these tales of old be acknowledged, what becomes of the very foundation of theology? For the whole scheme of the world, if you are to believe the teachers of that Old World in which my youth was passed, absolutely rests upon Adam and his fall, upon the Eve who was literally made out of one of his own ribs, upon the fatal apple, the speaking serpent, and the flaming sword! Conceive taking the foundation of theology from an old Turanian poem written a thousand years before Moses! Alas for the foundation of theology! Alas for any theology which is not founded on the ever-present Eternal! not founded directly upon the God in whom we live and move and have our being! But let us fairly acknowledge the consequences which will follow. If the infallibility of the Eden story in Genesis goes, the infallibility of all parts of the New Testament which are directly founded upon it also goes. The statement of 1 Tim. ii. 13, 14, that "Adam was first formed: then Eve; and Adam was not deceived, but the woman," can no longer be accepted as an infallible argument for the inferiority of woman. Deductions must be made even from Paul's grand argument in the Romans: "As by the offence of one man sin entered into the world, and death by sin." If the Eden narrative is not infallible, then Paul is not infallible. Once more, alas for a theology which vests infallibility in any man or in any book, and not in the infallible God alone!

But again: If the real original account of the deluge was in the eleventh book of an old Turanian poem, then you must make some abatement of the claim to infallibility of 1 Peter iii. 20: "The days of Noah, while the ark was preparing, wherein few, that is, eight souls, were saved through water," or of 2 Peter ii. 8: "God preserved Noah with seven others when he brought a flood upon the world of the ungodly," or of Hebrews xi. 7: "By faith Noah being warned of God concerning things not seen as yet, moved by fear, prepared an ark for the saving of his house," or of Matthew xxiv. 37, or Luke xvii. 26: "As it was in the days of Noah, so shall the coming of the Son of man be. They ate, they drank, they married, and were given in marriage, until the day that Noah entered into the ark, and the flood came and destroyed them all." What far-reaching consequences come from the rediscovery of Assyrian literature! The whole question of inspiration is reopened. These quotations alone are enough to show that the inspiration of Apostle and Evangelist did not prevent them from having the ideas current in their own time as to their ancient documents. Small wonder, then, that the theologians of the world into which I was born fought tooth and nail against the smallest introduction of new light and knowledge into the sphere of Biblical interpretation. For it is only fifty years since that time, and already some of their most cherished beliefs have received their death-wound.

This one instance out of multitudes which might be given is sufficient to show that infallibility is an impossible claim. Of course, if we think for a moment, the demand made upon Israel for a perfect revelation from beginning to end is not only a demand impossible but absurd. In a world that grows, growth is a part of true perfection. But if revelation grows, its first beginning must be small and its end vastly larger. The supreme glory of Israel's religion was that it grew. This is the true answer to such critics as Ingersoll. Israel was barbaric, was cruel, was she? Who informed you of the fact? Israel herself. Your ancestors and mine drank wine out of the skulls of their enemies less than a millennium and a half ago. What rescued them from their barbarism, their cruelty? Israel. Israel's last word, even barely half understood, came to Britain from Iona and Lindisfarne; came from Rome with Augustine, and instantly barbarism began to ameliorate and cruelty began to feel something of shame and self-reproach.

But there is another side to the question of Genesis. Once grant that the legends of the fall and deluge are not Israelitish but Turanian, and the original Hebrew inspiration is freed from the heavy load it has hitherto had to bear. For the supreme charm of Israel's prophecy is the forward not the backward look. It does not gaze sadly upon a lost paradise of yesterday, lost by man's sin; it looks forward to a paradise to be gained to-morrow, won by man's righteousness.

What, then, is the supreme glory of Israel's history? The discovery of God. Israel set herself the sacred task of discovering God and His relations to man. All the lines of Israel's religion converge here. Israel emerges out of the dim twilight of tradition at the exodus from Egypt. When we first catch a glimpse of the tribes in Canaan we see a dozen little tribal centres, so jealous of interference that nothing but the extremity of danger can unite them in a common action. The watchword which then rings out from Israel's gathered host is, "Jehovah, God of Israel." Jehovah's ark is Israel's standard. "Arise, Jehovah, and let thine enemies be scattered," is Israel's war-cry. This is the burden of the grand old song of Deborah, one of our most ancient landmarks. Now, whence did Israel derive this sense of unity? Surely not when the tribes were scattered among the hills of Palestine. No, the heroic age which united them in Jehovah's name dates certainly back to the exodus from Egypt, the march through the desert, and the advance upon Canaan. Thus we strike directly upon the great work of Moses. He is the maker of the nation. He fills them with belief in Jehovah, their deliverer; he leads them out of the house of bondage to the land of freedom in Jehovah's name, leaning on Jehovah's hand. What conception that great soul formed of Jehovah it is impossible to state; but what Israel's belief then and for ages afterward was is plain enough. Jehovah was the God of Israel. Says Jephthah to the leader of Moab, "You keep the land Chemosh your God gave to you; we shall keep the land Jehovah our God gave to us." Now, how did the thought of Jehovah expand? Each new seer added some new perfection by a new thrill of inspiration. Elijah stands for Jehovah's justice and purity. Jezebel's Baal was served by smiles and song, by bright processions of youths and maidens scattering flowers, and marching hand in hand to the temple of the god. But Baal was impure, sensual; Jehovah was pure and just.

But Elijah's Jehovah, though pure and just, was harsh and relentless to those who worshipped Him not.

Israel still ponders upon her great problem, and in the next age Micah sees that Jehovah requires of man to love mercy, as well as to do justice. Elisha followed up Elijah's war against the house of Ahab to the bitter end. He started and consecrated the bloody revolution of Jehu, and saw Jehu shed innocent blood like water, without one sign of disapproval. But Israel still ponders on her problem, and in the next age Hosea declares that Jehovah will visit the house of Jehu for the blood of Jezreel.

Again: very early did the wise men of Israel see a distinct connection between obedience to Jehovah and the prosperity of Israel. Their wise sayings are full of the direct connection between virtue and happiness, obedience and prosperity. But Israel still pondered her problem. And when bitter days came and misfortunes fell heaviest on the best and truest, such as Josiah and Jeremiah, the old solution was found not to fit the new facts. The author of the book of Job sees that God may give to the righteous man to drink of the cup of bitterness to the very dregs; and the Isaiah of the captivity rises to the height of this great argument when he sees that the ideal man is the suffering servant of God, the man of sorrows, who bears the griefs and carries the sorrows of weaker souls. By his stripes they are healed.

But now comes Israel's last, grandest, and hardest task, to make her ideal actual, to incarnate in flesh and blood the loving, suffering servant of God. And now she has to wait and work half a millennium, busied in the first attempt that ever was made to educate a whole people into righteousness. Only thus, by increasing the possibility of such a birth ten-thousandfold, can Israel succeed, if ever she does succeed. In the bitter times of exile, in the poverty-stricken days after the return, the finest hope of each of Israel's mothers was that from her the Deliverer might be born. A hope so radiant glorified all motherhood and cast a halo round all childhood. Israel kept expecting, praying, hoping that God would surely visit her and take away her reproach. And at last the Deliverer came. Sitting on the Mount of Galilee, Jesus sang at last the song of Israel's and the world's redemption. The Sermon on the Mount is Israel's last word. Freed at last from partiality, prejudice, narrowness, Israel chants, through the lips of Jesus, the strain of the love divine. Through him the Father is revealed. God is discovered at last. When man is seen to be God's child, man's true relation to God is finally and surely known.

CHRISTIANITY IN THE PRESENCE OF MODERN CRITICISM

BY REV. BROOKE HERFORD

OF BOSTON, MASSACHUSETTS

For a good many years there has been a vague impression abroad that modern criticism, if only men dared frankly face it, was very seriously undermining the whole position of Christianity. Thinkers who claimed to be advanced openly treated it as obsolete, or at least obsolescent. But a generation has passed and Christianity has not perished and does not seem perishing. It has changed, indeed, and broadened, but it seems as strong as ever. And people are beginning to wonder what all the criticism has come to? Were its anticipations a mistake, or has it never been really faced? How does Christianity stand in face of modern criticism?

Now, bear in mind the special point I have to deal with. I am not speaking of Religion in general. With regard to that, there can be little doubt. The tendency of the highest thought towards it is unmistakable. It has been questioned and investigated as never before, and in its fundamental elements—the being of God, and the higher nature of man, and man's immortality—it stands simply untouched.

But while Religion in its wide universal essence is thus safe, how is it with regard to Christianity? The place of Christianity has been as the clearest and divinest revealing of Religion. In it, that diffused light "which lighteth every man that cometh into the world" —all God's light—has seemed focussed into a clear, bright, helpful radiance in which men might rest their faith, and by which they might confidently live. There have, of course, been very great differences about it; all the way from regarding Christ as a great holy Teacher, to worshipping him as actually God. But the common ground which entitles all these differences to rank as Christianity is a special and unique reverence which has felt that, somehow, he stands at the Head of the world's religious life, that we may rest on his great teachings as on a rock, and that it is good to work and pray and organize our Religious life in his name.

Now, how has modern criticism affected all this?

There are three directions in which the fuller scholarship and keener thought of our time have been working on this problem of Christ and Christianity:

1. One line of criticism has been on the subject of Christ himself, as to whether we really know anything about him, and if so, what?

2. A second line has worked at Christianity; at the various systems called by that name,—trying to make out whether there really is any system distinct enough to be so named, and if so, what is it?

3. A third line has touched the deeper ground of man's own nature, and questions whether—even sup-

posing the world's reverence for Christ be just—still whether the attitude of discipleship, even to him, is not a mistake and the giving up of our individualism and freedom.

Now let us take these three points in their order.

1. As to how far modern criticism has affected our knowledge of what Christ really was, and what he taught. There is a wide-spread impression that the truer Biblical scholarship of to-day has been showing that in reality we know very little about Christ; that the Gospels instead of being almost contemporary accounts are only traditions, not written down as we have them till long afterwards; that consequently they cannot be depended upon; so that, in fact, all the seemingly clear outlines of that figure to which the world has been bowing down are melting away into a haze in which it is impossible to make out anything clearly. So you hear people say sometimes, that it is even doubtful whether any such person as Jesus ever really existed; and many imagine that anyhow there is very little known about him. But is this the result of modern criticism? I think I might say that the real result is almost exactly opposite to this. This was indeed what was at first announced as going to be the result. It is just fifty years since the great German critic, Strauss, startled Europe by his book on the life of Jesus. You know, it challenged the whole story of Christ. It evaporated the whole thing into a series of myths. Strauss supposed these myths to have grown up in the early Christian communities about the memory of a person who might indeed have lived, but had nothing of this remarkable kind about him.

Perhaps it was well that the very most that criticism could possibly do, should be thus announced at once. For it forced universal attention. It set every thinker in Christendom investigating the matter. Of course, timid people, ostrich-like, hid their faces in the sand, and would not admit that there was anything to be investigated. In the main, however, the facing of the question was fair and thorough. But what has been the result? Simply that that mythical theory has been practically rejected by the scholarship of the world. It was not large enough for the facts. That there are elements of myth in the Gospel narratives is likely enough; but that that is their main character, that such a portraiture should have formed itself about a mere commonplace life, was too impossible to be maintained. Nay, within four years Strauss himself had to modify his own theory, and pronounced that the Jesus about whom the myths had grown up must have been the supreme religious genius of the race. Well, the scholarship of the world, looked at broadly, may be said to have accepted that correction that Jesus must have been the supreme religious genius, and has been working ever since at the question of how far the accounts of him can be depended upon. And the result is about this: on the one hand, the old idea that the Gospels are inspired and infallible records, in which everything must be taken absolutely so,—that is practically gone. On the other hand, all idea that they are forgeries or "cunningly devised fables,"—that is all done away. What the real scholars of Europe and America have come to is about this: that the Gospels are the honest *bonâ-fide* accounts of Jesus as they were handed down among his disciples. Exactly how early they date is still unsettled. But this is noticeable: every discovery of late years has been in the direction of putting them a little earlier, not later than the first criticism supposed; and, whatever the exact date, this is coming out more and more clearly, that the main picture of Christ's life, in all its great moral and spiritual features, may be depended upon. You have to allow for mistake and exaggeration just as you have in reading the lives of Socrates or Alexander, and quite as often you have to allow for belittling, as the recollection of what he said and did passed through smaller minds; but when all that is done, the fact remains, and is coming out more clearly every day, that we have a fuller, more vivid picture of Jesus Christ than we have of any other life in the ancient world.

But, it may be said, if there is mistake and exaggeration, how can we separate the true from the false? Yet that is not really so difficult as it might seem. Because we know exactly the direction in which the exaggeration was going on all through the early centuries, and in the Gospels we see how little way it had got when they were written. The whole direction in which the image of Christ was being changed was that of increasing celestial glorification. You can trace the whole process. First they imagined a miraculous birth; then they made him out a sort of subordinate Divine Being; and gradually they fully deified him into that awful celestial Christ, the second person in the Godhead, whom the creeds expounded and the Church enthroned. But then there is just one good thing about all this glorification with

which the simple life of Jesus was overlaid. It was
like the dust and ashes which buried Pompeii, but in
burying it preserved it. The Church was so busy working out the celestial glory of Jesus, that the story of
the earthly life passed with little notice. It was hardly
meddled with at all. Thus you look behind all the
glittering christology and there that earthly life and
ministry remains, just in the simple stories of it as
they were told in the first days of all by some who had
even been companions of the master, and others who
had reverently remembered what they told. And so,
that central figure stands, its main features untouched
by criticism, that figure which has so strangely impressed itself on the heart of the world: Jesus of
Nazareth who went about doing good; with his great
thought of how the world might be the happy kingdom of God, and feeling it upon his soul from God to
proclaim it and try to draw men to it; Jesus of Nazareth with that simple, unconstrained loving-kindness
which drew to him those from whom others shrank
away; who went among sinners and outcasts, and
took up little children in his arms to bless them; Jesus
of Nazareth with his pure eyes that seemed to look
into the very face of God and see the realities of eternity; Jesus of Nazareth with his great, wise words of
duty, and kindness, and trust;—and all ending in that
cross, on which the light of holy love that glowed
through his whole life was focussed to an intense and
awful brightness. All this life and spirit of Christ
stands as firm and clear as ever. Criticism may show
that some of his words may have been dislocated, and
that some of the deeds may be doubtful; but the main

features of that great life, and its deep character and spirit, remain, really all the surer for the criticism.

2. Another line of criticism has been working, not so much at what Christ was, as at what his religion was. What is this Christianity which all are so anxious to claim? And criticism shows that there have been so many systems claiming to be Christ's, and, moreover, so many of his teachings which have also been taught by others, that it suggests the doubt whether there is really any system, any religion, which deserves to be called Christianity, and which is worth rallying to.

You know how this objection is constantly presented: "What is this Christianity which you want men to hold to, and for which you claim the highest place in human religion?" Says the critic: Do you mean the simple Christianity of the Catacombs, or the splendid ecclesiasticism of the Papacy? The Christianity of the Anglican Prelates, or of the Puritans whom they cast out, or of the Quakers whom both Prelatist and Puritans alike excommunicated? Do you mean the Christianity of the Sermon on the Mount, or of the Nicene Creed? Do you mean the Christianity of Calvin, or the Christianity of Servetus whom he burned? And when you have fixed on some one of these types will you tell us how much of its thought and of its ways you claim as distinctly Christian? Because there is a great deal that has commonly been ascribed to Christ which can also be found in other religions and other great teachers. The Vedic hymns sing of God as the "Universal Spirit;" Confucius has the Golden Rule; Marcus Aurelius teaches human brotherhood; and all religions have inculcated Charity. Define exactly what this Christianity is that you ask to have enshrined in the holy of holies of our reverence. And if you admit that you cannot define it, well, then, the critic says, we had better dismiss it. We cannot admit the claim of something that cannot be defined.

Yes; I know that seems very plausible, and yet it is all a delusion. Is a thing nothing because it cannot be defined? Why, there are many of the very greatest facts and forces, both in nature and in human life, that are entirely incapable of definition! Try to define the Gulf Stream. Nobody doubts that the Gulf Stream is a mighty reality, but who can define it? There is a vast current flowing through the ocean, and you know somewhere about where it comes from; and as it cleaves its way through the Atlantic the temperature is higher, and every land that it touches more fertile, and everything that comes within its sweep is carried on by its slow, strong, subtile force. No captain who sails the ocean but has to reckon with it. He cannot tell exactly where it begins or ends, or where its margin blends with the great ocean. He cannot define it, but what would you say of him if he, therefore, decided that it was not worth noticing?

Now it is something like that with Christianity, only in a larger, nobler fashion. Here, sweeping through the great world currents of these eighteen centuries is a mighty movement and force which history has called Christianity. You cannot define it. You know something of where and how it started. You can see something of what has been its character and direction. You know that it has made many a bleak shore fertile, though you may not be able to point to a single growth of institution or idea that has been due to it alone; and you see that it has carried forward the movement of the race, though you cannot absolutely distinguish its force from the other forces of progress.

I do not put this as an argument for bowing down to the mere name, Christianity, without trying to have a clear idea of the thing. No! but it is good for this, that we are not to let our natural estimation of it and our attitude towards it be affected by the criticism that it cannot be defined. You cannot define it, but you can see enough to judge of the extraordinary power there must be in it to be still mingling strongly with the currents of the world; you can see enough to judge of the direction of that power, that it is working towards goodness and kindness and helpfulness, and love to God and man; you can see enough, too, to enable you to trace it to its source in the life and ministry of Christ, and there you find it in a simplicity which there is no mistaking. There you see the few great truths which he himself preached as the Religion which might save the world. I know that this is very different from many of the systems which have claimed the name. It is something simpler and kindlier and more reasonable than almost any of them. You find there no such claims of empire as built up the Papacy. You find there no such iron-clamped dogmatizing as built up Calvinism. You do not find either the pomp of Anglicanism, or the clipped narrowness of Puritanism. Nay, you do not find many of the doctrines on which all these have agreed. When once you recognize it as a true principle of criticism to go back to Christ himself for the pure essence of Christianity, you have no more perplexity over the doctrine of the Trinity, for Christ never said a word about it; it was simply one God, the Heavenly Father, whom he preached to men. You find nothing in his teachings about Original Sin, or the total depravity and ruined helplessness of man; on the contrary, he always addresses men as having good in them as well as evil, and is always appealing to that good in them. So again in him there is nothing of the scheme of Substitution, it is simply Repentance and Amendment that he preaches, as the satisfaction that God's justice requires. And though we do find in him the sternest warnings of the future punishment of sin, it is not that hopeless eternity of torment into which his words have been hardened by the creeds; it is retribution administered and folded in by infinite Love. It is these few great thoughts of simple piety to God and love to man, of brotherhood, and kindness, and eternal life which constitute the original Christianity that started that great new current of onward and upward life, which we can thenceforth trace, though we may not be able to define it.

Then criticism comes in again, and says, "But even these teachings were not new; they have been thought and said by other teachers too." Well, but why should his teachings be entirely new? How could they be? There are no new truths! The truths of God, the duties of man, are as old as Creation! The supreme value to the world of Christ's teaching of those truths lay in the force with which his teaching of them went forth into the life of mankind. And that is a simple matter of fact. Those Vedic Hymns sang of the one Infinite Spirit, and men by and by forgot; the great thought died. Christ said "God is a Spirit," and the world has never forgotten it, and that word has been a life-force ever since. Marcus Aurelius talked beautifully of kindness and forgiveness, and though he had the prestige of an emperor, the world of Rome moved on and took no heed. Jesus of Nazareth said—only the same things, if you will—with no prestige at all, and a few lowly hearts were touched with a power which thrilled through that same great world of Rome, gave a new turn to history, and is still working, a live, real force, to-day.

3. There is yet one other line of criticism which touches the question of special discipleship to Jesus Christ. It is a subtler criticism than any relating to the records of Christ, or the definitions of Christianity. I speak of the modern criticism of man's own religious needs and power. It is the criticism which says, man must work out his own thought and faith; he must not sit at any one's feet, nor follow any master, nor commit himself to the side of any system. You know that attitude. This is the age of individualism. The greatest teaching of our modern prophets is to stand on one's own feet, to look out of one's own eyes, to trust one's own reason, to live out one's own life before God. Now, it is urged that the whole idea of special discipleship to Christ is a weak giving up of this individualism. All this talk of "sitting at the feet of Christ," of owning any "authority" in him, of calling him "Lord and Master," and loving to work and pray and carry our associated religious life "in his name," is objected to by this criticism as an essentially wrong attitude. It is not that those who take this attitude are at all indifferent to religion; but they say,

look into your own soul for your religion, not to Christ or any one else. Many of them feel the holy beauty of Christ's life, but still they object to this putting of him to the front. They think it is a mere piece of sentiment, if not a mere piece of superstition. Whatever you find of good and true in him, by all means take it, they say, but take it as your own thought, not as resting in him for it.

Now, I know that all this is apt to seem the true tone of mental freedom, and it especially claims to be the scientific method. But it is not really the scientific method. It is not the way in which man learns any knowledge and makes way to more knowledge and higher attainment. Men do not work, at first, at any rate, individually. They do not dig out their knowledge for themselves. Some things are settled, not to be perpetually reopened. A few great ones are the teachers, the authorities to the rest. From those authorities we learn the groundwork. We study with them at our side. The great scientists, the great artists, the great musicians,—we sit at their feet, we own them as our masters, we try to imbue ourselves with their spirit. Instead of divesting ourselves of any personal relation, we cultivate it all we can. Do you want your boy to be interested in science? Give him an hour with some enthusiastic naturalist. Let him wander through the woods with some one who knows and loves the flowers and even the beauties of the wayside weeds; or let some astronomer show him the stars through his telescope and tell him things about them which he would never find out for himself in the world, but which he implicitly takes in. The word made flesh—even the mere scientific word made flesh—is worth a hundred times over the same word only made into a book. Or do you want to foster the love of music? you gather your musical association together in some great name, of Mendelssohn or Beethoven. Or do you want to foster some fine public spirit? you band together under the standard of some great personal memory, or personal leadership. Is this the refuge of weakness, afraid to stand alone? No! it is the way of Nature—that is, of God—to help us to a finer strength, by drawing us together.

It is the personal leaderships which give in every part of life the intensest inspiration and the clearest point. It is simply the same in religion as in every other part of life. Why, every Grand Army Post rallying round the name of some old honored leader answers this criticism which would forbid the grouping of religious life about the thought and name of Christ. And so this clinging of our religious life to him, this loving to hold up his words before us, this sense of a revealing and authoritative light in his thought of divine things, this feeling of its being good to weave in the symbols of his name and work and cross into our worship and our work,—this, too, is not the refuge of religious weakness: it is God's provision to help us to religious strength.

And it does help us,—helps us in many ways, and I will close by speaking of a few of these.

For one thing, it keeps our faith more steadfast,— helps us to feel that we may count some things settled. If I am to depend simply on my own discerning of religious things, there are times when I seem to see clearly, but there are other times when I can see nothing, and if my own seeing were all, I should be apt to sink into utter doubt or disbelief. But with this great master, holding his hand, even though I am in darkness, I know the light is there.

And so I think, too, that this distinct discipleship to Christ gives strength and patience to our moral effort. Standing alone, what are we in this mighty conflict against wrong and sin? But in that leadership of Christ I feel the touch of all that long line who, through the ages, have still rolled on the tide of the world's forward battle. I am one with the shadowy millions of his followers. And so I take my part more hopefully, I hold on in it more confidently, I know the Lord's victory at last is sure.

And just one other help: I think that this distinct discipleship to Christ lifts us out of all small self-consciousness. Self-consciousness is the bane of life. I am bidden to work out my own thought, and to hold it because it is mine. That is the very thing I do not want to do. I do not want to think of my great trust in God and heaven and duty as *my* thought. I do not want to feel it something that just *I* have seen and set up for myself. When I do think of it that way, I distrust it. I want to rise above that. I want to feel that I am joining in with my fellow-men. I want simply to share in the greatest life of the race. I want to feel just as one of a great family clasping the feet of God, and treading together the ways of the immortal life. And in this leader of all souls it is just this great fellowship I feel, and in which I most lose myself, and rise into something of that loftier faith and spirit which, in him, I am looking to and trying to follow.

Yes! Here is the essence of it. Our best life is not that which we live alone, or which each age lives alone. Our best life is that in which we draw together; in which we link ourselves, and lose ourselves, in the great fellowships of the ages. And still, after all the keenest criticism of our questioning time, that fellowship which began in Christ, and still continues in his name, stands as the best. And though it is not all it might be, it is the best thing in the world to-day, and in "his name" through all its divisions preserves a latent bond of union, and a prophecy of how the union shall be fulfilled at last. So I would have us cherish this fellowship and the name which at once stands for it, and helps to keep it living. I would cherish it in our working; I would cherish it even in our praying. "In His Name;" it is no talisman to give some mystic efficacy either to the praying or the working, but it is a great strong name that links us with the noblest life that has been and that is. Yes! "In His Name!" that holds up before us the loftiest ideals; that stirs us to effort, and sacrifice, and patient service for the help of man; that gives to all our striving a special point and clearness; that is the perpetual reassurance of our faith, and that is the constant monitor to kindness and brotherliness, and all the most gracious piety and charity of life!

THE ETERNAL GOODNESS

BY REV. JOHN WHITE CHADWICK

OF BROOKLYN, NEW YORK

There are those who seem to think that when Jesus spoke of that divine tenderness which he felt supporting and enfolding him as his "Father" he was establishing a definition for all coming time. I cannot think that he had any such intention. Only in some way he must express the hope, the joy, the faith, that was in him. Some name he must give to the great Love which was the central fact of his experience, which met his thought and feeling turn whichever way he would and folded them like children to its heart. That this name, "Father," adequately expressed all that he felt, or that no other name would symbolize that thought so well for other men,—for any such interpretation of his words we have no warrant. Only, as from day to day and year to year he lived in the great warmth and comfort of an earthly father's love, and felt the blessing of his watchfulness and care, learning how steadily he meant his good when seeming most unkind, it was borne in upon his mind that however great and high the infinite love might be, surely it must be more like this than any other thing that he had known. The Church at almost every period of its development has left Joseph where the Madonna painters left him,—in the background. It has represented him as a stranger, an outsider, a mere looker-on. And it was as if Jesus, anticipating this age-long injustice, had set the seal of his condemnation on it, and instead of calling the Almighty Love by her dear name had called it exclusively by his. But be sure that if Mary was the mother that it seems she must have been to suckle such a child, in the inmost sanctuary of his life, where God was nameless ever, his thought of Him took color from her gentle eyes and tenderness from her embracing arms. So one who had in him more of the spirit that was in Jesus than any other person of our time, Theodore Parker, found his thought of God shaped by his mother's image, and was wont to pray, "O Thou who art our father and our mother!"

But it does not greatly matter by what name we call the All-Embracing Love. That we should feel and seem to know that there is such a love,—this is the all-important thing. Possibly we might get along without the name, without any name; to get along without the thing,—the man who can do that is less than human. We talk of Atheism much in these last days, and the word is one that drops with feathery lightness from our lips. "You know *I* am an Atheist," says Mrs. A. to Mr. B. between the oysters and the ices with a happy smile. But did there ever live a man or woman who could say it so with any real meaning in the words? What is called Atheism is oftenest the denial of a lower statement of the divine existence in the interest of a higher. But the vision of the Father which men crave is not comprised in any intellectual statement, however careful it may be. Show us the Father and it sufficeth us. So Philip cries in the New Testament narrative. So cries the universal heart of man. What is the real object of its cry? What is the real essence of this faith in God which we all want; which we may grow indifferent to in our folly and our sin, but to which in our shame and sorrow, and in every deepest hour, we cannot be indifferent; which at our best we hold a thing more precious than any other thing beneath the sun; which we would not lose, though losing it we should gain thereby a thousand lesser things,—what is the real essence of this faith?

It is belief in the essential soundness, in the eternal goodness of the world. Compared with this all matters of trinity or unity, of personal or impersonal deity, of Theism or Atheism, as these phrases generally go, are of little or of no account. Show us the Father and it sufficeth us. Show us the fundamental goodness of the world. Show us that God, or if there be no god, then that the universe is good. This is the saving faith. It is this which we must have or perish. It is not to be denied that one can live so superficially, so thoughtlessly, so drenched with comforts and delights, that these questions have for him no value and no interest. His business thrives, his home is beautiful, his wife devoted, his children happy, his health is excellent,—sufficient for the day is the good thereof. "To him who is well shod it is as if the earth were carpeted with leather." The healthy, prosperous man has better arguments than Leibnitz marshalled in his "Monadology" for an optimistic theory of the world. They are his good dinners and his good investments. That God is good is a deduction from these major propositions. But for the most part it is made unconsciously. There are many people who are too busy, or too happy, to give a moment's thought to matters of fundamental interest and importance. If they think at all concerning them, their thinking generally is that God must be good, He is so good to them; all must be well, all is so well with them. But there are many who do not think at all concerning ultimate things.

There are many, who do not, who would not be so happy as they are if once the question of the fundamental goodness of the world should meet them in some lonely, silent hour and look them fully in the face. For I am perfectly sure that even those who seem entirely satisfied with their own personal comforts and advantages, in many instances would find them dimmed and spoiled by even a suspicion of the fundamental soundness of the world. An underlying consciousness of this is the wide sea on which their many ventures sail with bellying canvas to and fro. It is the suppressed premise in the syllogism of their happiness. Convince them of its radical unsoundness and a blight would fall upon their every pleasure and success.

But there are also not a few for whom no personal advantages, no comforts or delights that wealth, or art, or love can press into their hands, can medicine into forgetfulness of "the deep things of God," the obstinate questionings of evil and of pain, the awful tragedies that afflict the course of nature and the life of man. For such there is no real happiness while these awful tragedies are unresolved, these questionings are waived aside, these deep things are not understood. No dull, half-sensuous consciousness of the eternal goodness will do for these. They cannot blind themselves to the enormous tragedy of nature and of human life. They must confront it open-eyed, must frankly question it and make it yield, if possible, some clear, intelligible reply. There are those who lack for nothing in the way of outward pleasure or success who are still far enough from being truly happy, because the burden of this mystery is too great for them to bear. Their honors and their joys, their fortunes and affections, are all infected by a cruel doubt whether, indeed, the eternal goodness is a substantial verity. And there are those, upon the other hand, who have a meagre share of outward blessings, who have had many losses and many great and dreadful sorrows in their lives, who, nevertheless, have an abiding happiness and an abiding peace, because somehow it has been made possible for them

> "To feel, although no tongue can prove,
> That every cloud that floats above
> And veileth love, itself is love,"

and to say with an afflicted one of old, "Though the Lord slay me yet will I trust in Him."

A consummation this which is devoutly to be wished. We do not want to be so sleek and comfortable that nothing of other men's sorrow and loss, and misery and pain, shall have for us any real existence. Nor do we want, once we are well aware how real these things are, to shut our eyes to them and stop our ears. We want to know the worst, though it should straightway spoil our every private joy. We want to know the worst if haply, knowing it, in spite of it and in equal spite of all that is most sad and tragical in our own lives, we may rest, as peacefully as ever in our mother's arms, in the persuasion that the love of God is infinite and everlasting, sufficient for all time and adequate to all events.

Show us the Father and it sufficeth us. Show us the eternal goodness and our joys will be transfigured with a holy light and our heaviest burdens we can somehow bear. There is no lack of circumstance to prove the power of the Eternal. The universe has been immeasurably enlarged to human apprehension by the advance of scientific knowledge. The new heavens and the new earth are infinitely greater than the old. But they have not increased in magnitude so much as they have increased in wonder. If the world of modern science is a thousand times more vast than the world of ancient thought, it is a million times more wonderful. But this revelation of immensity and wonderfulness is not sufficient for our deepest need. It is sufficient for the imagination, not for the conscience and the heart. Indeed, would not a God so infinite in power and wisdom, of whose beneficence we could not be sure, be less to us than one of attributes less awful in their majesty, if we could not confidently add to these the attributes of goodness and of love? Intellect, intelligence, genius, without love, was Hawthorne's favorite symbol of the perversion of humanity; it made the man a devil. Raise his conception to an infinite power, and still the essential truth of it remains. An infinitely powerful and intelligent and loveless God; could we imagine anything more horrible? Show us the Father and it sufficeth us. Show us the eternal goodness and we can bear our private griefs and losses, however dreadful they may be, and the great world-spectacle of misery and pain will not avail to make us wholly sad.

Nevertheless, we would not be of those for whom a currency of phrases seems to be a matter of the first importance. We want to have *our* phrases paper that is convertible at sight into the facts of our experience. To go on talking of the eternal goodness, while selfishly or wilfully ignoring the innumerable facts that seem to point a very different moral, is not the part of wise men, but of fools; neither the part of good men, but of base. Let us at least endeavor faithfully to see things as they are. In that preposterous story, "Mr. Isaacs," Ram Lal, the Esoteric Buddhist, generates an all-obscuring fog upon some critical occasion. Had it been a fog of words it would have been no miracle, or one that we have seen performed a thousand times. There are two phases of experience which we have got to reckon with in dealing with this matter of the eternal goodness. One is the infinity of suffering in the animal and the human world. The other is the absence of all supernatural interference with the habitual order of the world. As for the first, the development of scientific knowledge, on which we pride ourselves, has added many thousand illustrations. The cruelties, the rapacities, the malignities, that diversify the mutual relations of the individuals and families of the animal world are as conspicuous in the literature of natural history as the wars, political, religious, mercenary, that make the history of man "a fountain filled with blood." Hundreds of facts elucidated by the patience of the great biologists do not reveal the marvellous ingenuity of natural processes a whit more obviously than they reveal their hideous cruelty. The most ingenious devices are generally the most elaborately cruel. The terms that biological science has made most familiar—the struggle for existence, natural selection, the preservation of the fittest—epitomize events and processes that Torquemada and the Duke of Alva might have read about with growing self-respect. The literature of animal parasites and messmates is particularly instructive to investigators of the moral aspect of the world. It is intensely interesting reading, but is not immediately invigorating to our sense of the eternal goodness. There are some dozens of different varieties of these squatter sovereigns that deploy themselves upon different areas of the physical man; the liver, the intestines, the heart, the eyeballs, the lobes of the brain,—all have their parasites. The argument from design was formerly highly esteemed for the proofs it furnished of a beneficent Creator. But how about that hardy voyager who is so admirably adapted for getting into the stomach of the shark without injury to himself, and once there for cutting his way out,—having some artifice of revolving knives,—not without injury to the other party to this ingenious contrivance? The literature of insectivorous plants reveals the fact that the cruelty and rapacity and insidiousness of nature are not confined to animal and insect life. These traits are equally displayed by many vegetable forms. The pitcher-plant is so contrived as to souse the adventurous insect in a tiny bath, which causes instant death. It has little prickles which only make themselves felt when the insect attempts to go back, and then they render this impossible, and it has a sweetish fluid that entices the victim to enter the fatal tube. In other instances the ingenuity is more elaborate, and, if we were speaking of our fellow-men, we should say more diabolical. How fascinating were the milk-weeds you saw last summer as you walked or drove along, their purple blossoms colored with swarms of flying things! But their milk was not the milk of human kindness. It lured many a happy loiterer to his death, catching him by the proboscis as he tugged away, and holding him inexorably when he had had enough. These are but random instances out of a countless number that have been tabulated by the specialists who have vied with one another in the interpretation of the mysterious relationships of animal and insect life.

The insects are larger and the traps are different when we come to man's estate, but is the impression much more reassuring on the whole? Puncture the social origins of mankind at any point and there is a spurt of blood. Take a few sentences from the latest volume which has concerned itself with primitive society,—Mr. John Fiske's "Destiny of Man viewed in the Light of his Origin." "In respect to belligerency," he says, "the earliest men were doubtless no better than brutes." "To get food was the prime necessity of life, and as long as food was obtainable only by hunting and fishing, or otherwise seizing upon edible objects already in existence, chronic and universal warfare was inevitable. The conditions of the struggle for existence were not yet visibly changed from the outset in the animal world. That struggle meant everlasting slaughter, and the fiercest races of fighters would be just the ones to survive and perpetuate their kind. . . . That moral sense which makes it seem wicked to steal and murder was scarcely more developed in them than in wolves." And as the wolf, the lion, and the tiger fattened upon the spoil of their teeth, so did the primitive man upon the spoil of his hands. If you care to read a more dreadful and more loathsome chapter than that which treats of the primitive struggle for food, read one like that of Lubbock or McLennan, which treats of primitive marriage. Clubs, ropes, and stones, these were the only witchcraft that the Othellos of the early times used when they wooed the Desdemonas of some rival tribe or clan.

But it is by no means necessary for us to go back so far for facts that put a fearful strain upon our faith in the eternal goodness. The history of Christianity, with its various persecutions and religious wars, will serve us just as ill. The Spanish inquisition, the superstition of witchcraft and its accompanying horrors, these are affairs of modern times, but nothing that Tylor and Spencer and Lubbock and McLennan have written of man's earliest beginnings are so palsying and chilling to the heart. The apologetic theologian urges that these things are not divine, but human. God only permits them; He is not their cause. Cause or permission matters not to us. What God permits, for that He is responsible. And take any such gigantic horror, such as the witchcraft delusion or religious persecution, and how infinitesimal are the elements of conscious human wickedness in comparison with the great whole of irresponsible belief, as honest, as sincere, as any that has ever clouded or irradiated human thought. But we need not go back even to the sixteenth and seventeenth centuries for a sufficient trial of our faith. The incidents of our habitual life are manifold that furnish such a trial. What sufferings of the body and what torments of the mind have we not seen endured by men and women who would not knowingly have violated any law of human publication or divine! If we can still keep our faith in the eternal goodness in the face of all these things, it is well and good. But to ignore them is to convict ourselves of shameful ignorance, or of more shameful heartlessness.

Another thing, as I have said, with which we have to reckon in our dealings with this matter, is the absence of all supernatural interference with the habitual order of events. Faith in such interference has been the refuge of a countless host from the apparent ruin of their religious optimism by the appalling facts of animal and human sufferings. But the first instance of such interference has not yet been fairly proved. And if a thousand or a hundred thousand instances could be established of such interference,—to check the violence of superstition, to crown the righteous cause with victory, to rescue injured innocence, or to bring the cause of boastful wickedness to shame, to allay the sufferings of some agonized victim of intolerable pain, to chase away the phantoms that disturb the balance of the mind,—would the eternal goodness be in any least degree assured by such a grand array? To answer yes one must be most illogical, or most selfish it may be. The logical and unselfish answer is, If there have been so many instances of interference, why have there not been more? Why have so many been allowed to suffer nameless torments when such torments might have been allayed? Why have so many innocent and noble persons been allowed to go to the block, the gallows, and the stake, suffering more horribly from cruel and unjust suspicions than from the axe or flame? No; for the honor of the Eternal, let us be glad that it cannot be shown that He has ever interfered to stay one murderous stroke, to soothe one agonizing pang. Upon the train that rushes to destruction in another's fierce embrace two men sit side by side,—one of them rich and enriching others with a thousand golden deeds; the other foul and cruel utterly. Does the wreck assure the safety of the better man? Of neither probably, and possibly of the worse. We are all embarked on such a train. It rushes from the cradle to the grave. The catastrophe is the universal pain and sorrow of mankind. It is no respecter of persons. Cry as we will for God to rend the heavens and come down, the azure vault still keeps itself unbroken and impervious to our prayer.

Nothing is more pathetic in the history of human thought than the attempts which men have made to keep their faith in the eternal goodness in despite of the portentous shocks it has received from the phenomena of human misery and the tragic elements in every form of sentient life. In view of these phenomena and these tragic elements, John Stuart Mill expressed astonishment that a dualistic theory of the world had not been more favorably received. But what theory of the world has been received more favorably? Within Christian limits certainly the devil has been as objective to men's thought and feeling as God. For many centuries did not men's thought and action have much greater and more frequent reference to the Devil than to the Deity? Here was a theory of the world that permitted men to still hold fast their faith in the eternal goodness, no matter what calamity or ruin or distress should come upon them. As the piano-tuner had his *wolf* into which he swept all the discords of his instrument, so the theologian had *his* wolf, his devil, into which he swept all the discords of the universe. The most serious trouble with this kind of thinking was, that if it proved that God was good, or might be so in spite of all the cruel discords of the world, it also proved that He was good for nothing; certainly not for much. Oftener than not He seemed to get the worse of the unending fight.

But the devil-explanation of the pain and various evil in the world has ceased long since to be entirely, or even tolerably, satisfactory to the majority of thoughtful men. Unconscious cerebration has effected the most of this important change, but of conscious thinking there has been no serious lack, and the result of this has been as follows: either, God being infinite, the devil is His devil, and He is finally responsible for all his works and ways, or, if this be not so, then God is not infinite, and whether good or evil is the dominant factor in the universe, it is impossible for us to decide. The first conclusion does not help at all; the second is one in which no thoughtful person can rest for a day, no, not for an hour. The devil-explanation having been disgraced, another thrust itself into the vacant seat: the Relativity of Human Knowledge. This formula, which is not without validity in a certain sense, was so interpreted as to mean that God may be good and yet not be what we should mean by "good" were He our fellow-man. One sentence of John Stuart Mill's did more to put this notion to an open shame than any other; than all others I am inclined to say: "I will call no being good who is not what I mean when I apply this epithet to my fellow-creatures, and, if such a being can sentence me to hell for not so calling him, then to hell I will go." Those to whom Mill opposed himself had said that the character of God was not such as could be sanctioned by "the highest morality we are capable of conceiving." The short of this was, "Evil, be thou my good." If we can only hold that God is good by calling evil by another name, the time has come for the Promethean taunt, "I reverence thee! Wherefore?"

How then? Bereft of those devices which in the nearer or remoter past have enabled men to still maintain at least a *quasi* faith in the eternal goodness, while frankly recognizing how much misery and tragedy there is in nature and in human life, is nothing left for us, confronted by these often dreadful, sometimes hideous and appalling facts, but to succumb to them? That God is good, that God is Love,—must these time-honored predications be henceforth a mockery? Must we endeavor to surround ourselves with every comfort and felicity if haply in the near and present joy we may forget the great world-pain, and numb ourselves into indifference whether there is good or evil, love or malignity, at the heart of things? We could not if we would: the pain and misery press too close and hard for any such solution. They break down all the barriers of success and comfort we oppose to them, and look out on us from faces dearer to us than life itself.

> "There is no flock, however watched and tended,
> But one dead lamb is there;
> There is no fireside, howsoe'er defended,
> But has one vacant chair."

We would not if we could. It would be a cowardly retreat; a dastardly surrender. No, we will not blind and deafen and benumb ourselves to human misery, or to the misery of any living thing. "Never will we seek private individual salvation. Never will we enter into final peace alone." So said the Buddhist votary. So say we, each and all. Show us the Father and it sufficeth us. But if this vision is denied, if we cannot say as many millions have believed so fondly, that God is good, that God is love, then we will bear our burden as we can; that *man* is good, that *man* is love, do what we can to show.

This if the worst should come. But the worst has not yet come. It is still far remote, and is receding with each new advance of modern thought. There is no phrase in modern literature that resumes so much of what is best in modern science and philosophy as the phrase of Matthew Arnold,—The Power, not ourselves, that makes for righteousness. What currency it has had, what approbation! How it has been taken up and echoed and re-echoed by thinkers of the most different schools and tendencies of thought! And, what ample justification it has had from the most comprehensive studies of the fortunes of mankind, from the far-off beginning of its upward climb! What do the centuries thunder so loudly, whisper so silently, as the indifference of the Eternal to anything but the best that man can do or be? There is a Power, *not ourselves*, that makes for righteousness. Doubtless there is a power that is ourselves that makes for righteousness. But there is more than this, more than the consensus of the competent, more than the aggregate of human tendencies or wills. The whole creation, said the apostle, "groaneth and travaileth in pain together until now . . . For the earnest expectation of the creation waiteth for the manifestation of the sons of God." What rude anticipation here of the most lofty and inspiring thought of modern times! The stream cannot rise higher than its fountain. Because goodness, righteousness, is that for which all human centuries have yearned, we know that the unhuman centuries that went before yearned for the same result, we know that wallowing saurians and gigantic ferns, and fiery nebulous matter, thrilled to this music though they knew it not, we know that the Eternal loveth righteousness, is righteous; ay, that God is good. That which is the end of life must be its great original. It is impossible that God, the universe, should make such a demand for goodness and yet should not be good. "Can mortal man be more just than God?" It is unthinkable. And being so, all human goodness is a pledge that God is good.

But not more certain is it that there is a power not ourselves that makes for righteousness, for goodness, than that there is a power not ourselves that makes for love. "Love is the fulfilling of the Law." It was said originally of the Jewish ritual law. How much more grandly is it true of the law of universal progress, the law of universal life! "For surely," one has said, "if the choicest thing which the universe produces is love, then love must be that in which the life of the universe consists." Do men gather grapes of thorns, or figs of thistles? No! and therefore verily because the fairest flower and soundest fruit in all the world is love, what except love can be the root and seed? What can we be so certain of as this,—that God is Love?

There is simply no escape from these conclusions. The tendency of all things, and the ends to which they tend, are final testimonies of the goodness and the loving-kindness of that Eternal Life from which all things proceed. But still the facts of pain and misery recur. What shall we say to them, if haply we may rank ourselves with those

> "Who trust that God is love indeed,
> And Love creation's final law,
> Though Nature, red in tooth and claw
> With ravine, shrieks against their creed,"

and though "the still, sad music of humanity" pleads to the same effect? Now God be thanked, and many men with Him, that there is that in modern thought which, if it does not utterly abate the horror of the darker side of nature and of human life, gives us at least another point of view from which this darker side is seen shot through and through with arrows of immortal light. So long as the Creator theory of the universe prevailed and the argument from design was used to bolster up its tottering majesty, so long as the divine activity was thought about as something long ago suspended, the world as something long ago complete, men (the more thoughtful) might well bruise themselves to death against the bulk of natural and human misery. The argument from design was a two-edged sword, and often hurt the bearer more than those whom he opposed. For there proved to be a thousand and ten thousand truly exquisite adaptations which those who had the honor of the Almighty in their keeping could not endure to think were specially designed. But a different face is put at once on this whole matter the moment we perceive that the order of Nature and Humanity is not a completed fact, but a self-regulating tendency, and that this tendency has an invariable sweep, so far as we can see, towards the amelioration of all vital and social conditions. We wonder at those great cathedrals at which, century after century, men have wrought with loving patience, and which still remain unfinished. But here is this great world-cathedral, so vast that the planet on which we live, with all its marvellous mountain buttresses, and all its flowing tracery of clouds and streams, and all its infinite wealth of human love and joy, is less in comparison with the whole than one faithful chisel-stroke in comparison with the whole marvellous structure of Milan or Cologne, and this great world-cathedral has been building millions and billions of years, and we stand day after day in its stupendous nave, and night after night look up to its majestic starlit roof with steady pulse and unabashed demeanor. But now supposing that soon after the work on the great cathedral of Cologne came to a stop, some one had arrived upon the ground and had proceeded to criticise the edifice in its incomplete condition, as if it had arrived at its completion. And if he should be anxious to establish a belief of its perfection for himself and others to what ingenious theories he would be compelled to resort to justify the various incongruities, the transept all untouched, the arrested towers, the broken traceries, the great heaps of rubbish lying all about, and the great stagings that cumber the interior and cling to the external walls. Not otherwise is the ingenuity of those who from a world that is still in process of development argue as from a world mechanically finished and complete. The hard is still hard, the pain is still pain, the misery is still misery, the tragedy is still tragical enough, but it does make a world of difference whether the hard, and painful, and miserable, and tragic things are all finalities or necessary incidents of a process which has been from bad to good, is now from good to better, and must go on from better to the best. Surely, in such a scheme of thought, though there is nothing that can make our pains and losses wholly void (and how we should rebel against it if it could!), there is something that can sustain and tranquillize our thoughts, something that makes it possible to say, whatever graves may open at our feet, "Though the Lord slay me yet will I trust in Him!" "The cup which my Father hath given me shall I not drink it?"

But when Philip said to Jesus in the New Testament narration, "Show us the Father and it sufficeth us," it is set down that Jesus answered him, "He that hath seen me hath seen the Father." I doubt if Jesus answered Philip so. I do not doubt that he might so have answered him in all sincerity. How then? Was Jesus God? No, if there is an atom in the universe that is not God. Yes, if all things, all men, are parts of His infinity. "He that hath seen me hath seen the Father:" so any man might say whose mind and heart were full of truth and love. Hath seen the *Father!* Not merely a reflection of His essential character, but a manifestation of Himself. And there is no other manifestation of the Father that is so good as this. Nothing is so convincing to us of the eternal goodness as the goodness of our fellow-men; nothing is so convincing to us that God is love as the love that beams for us in the fond eyes of those whom we love best. Nothing, did I say? But there is one exception, and it is of the first importance. Not from without, but from within proceeds the surest revelation. Not the good offices that we receive, but the good offices that we bestow assure us most profoundly of the essential soundness of the world, convince us of the goodness and the love of God. Blessed are the pure in heart, for they shall see Him as He is. To the pure He will show Himself pure, to the merciful He will show Himself merciful, and to the upright man He will show Himself upright. But when we have attained to this beatitude, we shall not only show the Father to ourselves but to our fellow-men.

Honor to all the saints of long ago and now; to all the spirits true and tried who, by their manly strength and womanly devotion have made it possible for us to believe in God, the Father, even when sorrows black as night and terrible as hell threaten to make all goodness and all love seem but a mockery! Honor to those whom we, ourselves, have known as good and true as any of the best of old! Thanks for all such, but deepest thanks of all for that beatitude which Jesus promised to the pure in heart, which has been verified a hundred thousand times, a thousand million times, since it was spoken eighteen centuries ago. It is well for us if we can follow reverently in the steep track of those who from the mountain-top of Science see the mighty sweep of the eternal purpose, from the fire-mist to the polyp, and from the polyp to the saint. It is better for us if we have known and loved, been cherished by and cherished, men and women of such abounding goodness that under its exalting influence it was impossible for us to doubt the final goodness of the All. But it is best of all for us if we have kept our individual hearts so clean and bright that they are as a mirror in which we behold the eternal goodness, and not only we, ourselves, but those whose creed is daily bettered by our deed.

> "Patience! God's House of Light shall yet be built,
> In years unthought of, to some unknown song,
> And from the fanes of Science shall her guilt
> Pass like a cloud. How long, O Lord, how long?—
>
> "When Faith shall grow a man, and Thought a child,
> And that in us which thinks with that which feels
> Shall everlastingly be reconciled,
> And that which questioneth with that which kneels."

THE DEBT OF RELIGION TO SCIENCE

BY REV. MINOT J. SAVAGE

OF BOSTON, MASSACHUSETTS

BETWEEN a knowledge of the laws of God (which is Science) and a reverent and loving obedience to the laws of God (which is Religion), it seems simply and only absurd to suppose the possibility of any conflict. Yes, to us, who have outgrown that state of mind to which such an antagonism seemed not only natural, but inevitable, it does seem very absurd. But, of course, it has not seemed absurd to those who have believed it in the past; it does not seem absurd to those who still believe it to-day. To them, on the other hand, the very title of this address would be an absurdity. Religion indebted to Science? Rather would they hold it true that Science is the modern antichrist, "that opposeth and exalteth himself against all that is called God or is worshipped; so that he sitteth in the temple of God, setting himself forth as God" (2 Thess. ii. 4). Science, they say, is the enemy of revelation; it opposes knowledge to faith; it encourages doubt in the presence of divine mysteries; it impeaches the accuracy of the Bible; it denies the fall of man; it refuses credit to the miraculous; it questions the use of prayer; it casts a mist of uncertainty over the future destiny of man; it puts force and law on the throne of the universe, and declares that God is an unneeded hypothesis. It discredits the whole scheme of salvation, and leaves man " without God and without hope in the world."

Such is the way in which science is looked upon by the rigorous and consistent champions of the old faith. And among thousands, who do not openly oppose or impugn the methods and results of modern knowledge, there is an uneasy feeling that its tendencies are dangerous to religion; and they wonder if the battle now raging be not the real Armageddon, long ago foretold, in which is to be fought out the final great conflict between God and His enemies. It is not at all inconsistent with this state of mind that these men should declare, as did Mr. Talmage in his Philadelphia lecture, " There is no contest between genuine science and revelation." For, with these, "genuine science" is only such science as does not conflict with their view of revelation. In this way, any most bitter opponents can be brought into the most loving harmony.

But, instead of ridiculing or denouncing the opposition to science of these old instituted religions, it is more important that we understand it. After recognizing the facts, if we can find out how such states of mind came to be facts, we shall then be ourselves fitted to do something toward bringing about a better comprehension of the real relation in which science stands to religion.

At the outset, then, we note the fact that most of the leading scholars and scientific men of the world do not believe in the historic creeds of the popular Church.

Now and then there is an exception in the case of a scholar whose studies do not lead him on to controverted ground; or there is a scientific man, like Faraday, who, as if he were handling explosive gases, avowedly keeps his science and his religion carefully apart from each other. But the general statement is true. And the religious leaders naturally infer that, in scientific studies that lead to such results, there must be something essentially hostile to religion. The general antagonism seems proved, then, by patent facts; and, when we come to look beneath the surface, we find the undercurrents of spirit and method to be sweeping in different directions. Free thought, investigation, doubt, and the demand for proof,—these are of the very soul of science. But the official exponents of religion teach that the first step toward God is a childlike spirit of belief, the unquestioning acceptance of what is unhesitatingly taught. The New Testament declares that " he that believeth and is baptized shall be saved; but he that believeth not shall be damned." And Thomas, who did nothing worse than ask proof in support of the claim that a stupendous miracle had been wrought, is held up to peculiar reprobation. To-day, we should reprobate the man who was so credulous as to do anything else. It is, indeed, admitted that the dogmas of religion appear to be incompatible with reason. Therefore, reason is denounced; and faith is taught as a superior faculty, that is able to grasp facts that are above reason. Reason and faith, therefore, are often regarded as polar opposites. Not long ago, a leading ecclesiastic of Boston said to me, " It is either reason or faith. Were it not for my faith in the Church, I should be where you are." And this peculiar "faith" no one claims to be able to substantiate by the scientific method. Popular religion decries "the wisdom of this world;" and the Prayer Book asks us to renounce "the world and the flesh," as well as "the devil." And, in common religious phraseology, there is a "God of this world," who is supposed to be the great opponent of the God of religion. But this world is the sacred text-book of all scientific study.

Such, then, being the general mutual attitudes of science and instituted religion, it is not strange that the majority of preachers regard the tendencies of modern thought with suspicion. It is not strange that a minister should privately tell a friend that he did not allow himself to read any book that threatened to disturb his belief. I remember that, when I was first beginning to be looked upon as a heretic, one of the principal charges against me was that I had so many scientific books in my library. Out of such study no good could be expected. It is perfectly natural that the late pope, Pius IX, should turn the artillery of the Vatican against modern knowledge. It is perfectly natural that the drift of all modern literature, and that the influence of the common schools, should be looked upon with alarm. It is perfectly natural that professors in theological seminaries should be driven from their chairs for teaching evolution.

These are not peculiarly modern facts. Neither are they accidental. The long warfare of the Church against free thought and natural knowledge is familiar to you all. To detail it would be to review church history for the last eighteen hundred years. And this, as

I have said, is no accident. The spirit of investigation and proof seems to have been as utterly foreign to the mind and method of Jesus as to any of his followers. Indeed, there is no trace of it in the Bible anywhere. Throughout the Old Testament, it is the seer and the oracle that are looked to as the sources of all knowledge. Indeed, this age-long antagonism appears at the very beginning; for the primal sin, followed by the primal curse, was tasting the fruit of "the tree of knowledge." The Elohim seem to have been jealous lest "the man become as one of us." In almost all the great religions the gods are easily offended, easily made jealous of man. They look with suspicion upon his attempts to become wise or to better his physical condition. Utter humility and prostration, poverty and self-deprecation, have always pleased them better. What else but this is the lesson of the Prometheus myth? Jove is angry because the old Titan has shown pity toward the abject condition of the despised human race. In most of the great religions the supreme gods have shown themselves friendly toward men, if at all, only through some mediator or intercessor. For some reason or other there is almost always enmity. The search for knowledge and the attempt to produce a higher worldly civilization are treated as impiety.

Now, for a fact so wide-spread as this we have been considering, there must exist some equally general cause. And this cause, it seems to me, is not very far to seek. It would take me too long to trace the processes by which it has come about; but, in perfectly natural ways, it has come to pass that God has been set over against matter as its eternal opposite. It is spirit *and* matter, God *and* nature; and the two are in everlasting contrast. The root of the opposition is in the philosophy which underlies our conceptions of both religion and science. The leaven of Manichæism still works in the modern world. We escaped the outright dualism of the Avestan faith. Young Christianity was wise enough to reject the extremest folly of the Gnostics, who held to an almost impassable gulf between God and the world, even denying that the pure, supreme Spirit could have condescended to create it at all. But, practically, the dominant Christian philosophy has come to substantially the same thing. God's kingdom has not been treated as the natural product, the consummate flower of this world's growth in civilization. Rather is it true that this world has been regarded as alien from God, an opposing kingdom, in revolt against Him, separated from His divine life, and tending evermore to deeper degradation. The Christian in this world is in an enemy's country: he must fight all natural tendencies, and hold himself aloof from all worldly entanglements. In this way, he may one day escape from the prison-house of the flesh, and be received into God's eternal kingdom of spirit. God, then, is outside the world and opposed to it. His elect ones are chosen out of it; and, when the process of their training, through temptation and sorrow, is completed, He will burn it up. Then His kingdom of spirit will be forever separated from all those who have been the children of this rebellious world.

With a dominant philosophy like this, it could not be otherwise than that religion should find an apparent enemy in science. Knowledge of a ruined, fallen, accursed world, a world at enmity with God, could not do other than lead its devotees away from God. And, when this knowledge began to teach doctrines opposed to what was firmly held to be a supernatural and divine revelation, this only served to confirm the opinion that it was the enemy of God. Worldly wisdom could not be expected to discover revealed truths, and it was not competent to judge them. It was treated, therefore, only as a self-willed refusal of rebellious natures to bow to righteous and just authority.

But the devotees of science have kept on their humble, common-sense way, until they have accumulated so vast a body of verifiable natural knowledge that it can no longer be disregarded. It has changed the face of the earth, and lifted the level of human life. However it may have damaged man's prospects for the next world, it has unspeakably benefited this one. And, at the same time, its results in the realm of thought have been such that the old religious beliefs are fast fading from the minds of intelligent men. So a problem faces us. What does the attitude of the modern world mean? Is God being defeated in His attempt to govern the world? Or is it not more probable that His self-constituted interpreters have mistaken the relation in which He stands to it? Is it not just possible that God is in the world, not outside of it? and that He is leading it forward, not fighting against its progress? This seems to be, at any rate, the growing conviction of the grown-up humanity of the nineteenth century. And, at least, it may be worth looking at before rejecting it in the interest of the childish fancies of the world's ignorant and inexperienced childhood. Let us, then, look a little at this matter of science, and see what it is.

Since Science won her first and most dramatic triumphs on the fields of physical research,—such as astronomy, geology, and chemistry,—there is a feeling in the popular mind that the physical is her peculiar and only proper sphere. And certain other claimed methods of knowledge appear to be very jealous lest she should get out of this sphere. But she has already asserted her right of eminent domain in biology, in anthropology, in sociology; and she already promises to bring order out of confusion in ethics, and is beginning with her methods to explore the mysteries of religion. And her claim is nothing less than "Everything or nothing." Meantime, the other so-called methods claim to be able to put us in possession of certain most important kinds of knowledge to which the plodding feet of Science can never lead. They have turnpikes, cross-cuts, "royal roads"; they soar on quick wings, while Science, like a grub, only burrows in the earth. So they tell us.

Let us look, then, a little at these other methods, and see if their claims are good. Faith is one of these. But what is faith? As very commonly used, it is only credulity. Faith can have nothing to do with questions of history, as to whether such or such a thing really happened at some time in the past. That is a question of evidence. Neither can faith rightly concern itself with the truth or falsity of certain dogmas that offer themselves for belief. All true faith must base itself on and spring out of human experience. In the light of the past, and following the trend of what has been, it reaches forward beyond the visible, and grasps as real that which is not yet seen. It finds its reason and justification, as we shall soon see, only in science. Supernatural revelation, again, claims to be another source of knowledge. But, were there any such thing, it would have—before it could be cognizable by man—to come within the range of and submit to be judged by human experience. It falls definitely within the scope, then, of the scientific method. No matter what its source or nature, it can reach and touch man only as it becomes a fact in his experience; and, as such, it must be dealt with. So far as it transcends experience, it is outside of and beyond our range, and so far unknown; and, if we are to accept its credentials, they must be submitted to us for examination and verification. Supernatural revelation itself, then, must submit itself to the scientific method before it can be of any use to us. Another supposed source of knowledge is intuition, the quality or gift of the seer, the direct insight of supersensible truth. But, so far as intuition is real, Science adopts and explains it, making easy room for it as one form of the first step in her own true and only method of knowledge.

As a concrete illustration of what I mean, let us take him who is regarded as the greatest seer of our modern world,—our Emerson. He says, "I see: the truth looks to me so and so." But he positively disclaims argument or proof. What, then, is this seeing of his? No matter that he uses the "mind's eye" instead of the physical organ of vision, his seeing is neither more nor less than observation, the first step in the scientific method. And no matter how true or grand his seeing, just because he does not take the other steps of the process of science, his seeing is wholly useless to me, unless I also can see the same. Suppose I say, "I see a mast far off on the edge of the horizon at sea." But you are short-sighted,

and do not see it. You have, then, only my bare word
for it; and it is open to you to suppose it only a fancy
on my part, or traceable to some defect in my own vision.
So this kind of seership is grounded only on personal
authority, and there is no way of making it certain to
one who is inclined to doubt. This kind of wisdom is
non-transferable. And, the minute you take steps to
prove it, you do so, and must do so, by going on to complete the processes of the scientific method. So of philosophy: it is not an independent method or source of
knowledge, and it is valid only as it uses scientifically
ascertained truths as its subject-matter, and deals with
them in accordance with the scientific method.

To make clear and to substantiate these points, let us
turn to, and note carefully what we mean by the scientific method. It consists of three steps or processes:
1. Observation; 2. Hypothesis; 3. Verification by fresh
and repeated observation and experiment. If we take
only the first step,—observation, or looking,—what we
think we see may be only an illusion, a partial or erroneous impression, due to some carelessness on our part
or to some personal defect. It is only when we have
corrected and verified our impressions by repeated experiment that we can be reasonably sure of what we call
knowledge; for most of our first impressions are more
or less erroneous. The very first observation may be
correct and complete; but on that basis alone we can
never be sure of it.

The thing we claim to see by faith or intuition, the thing
that philosophy or revelation claims to bring before us
as real,—this thing may be real; but we can never thus
be certain of it. We have no right to call it knowledge

until we have subjected it to renewed experiment, and have verified it. In this way, and in this way only, can we prove that it is not due to some subjective illusion or to some personal peculiarity or defect of observation.

And the distinction which is commonly set up between so-called physical knowledge, to which the scientific method is appropriate, and another so-called spiritual knowledge that transcends the scientific method, is wholly unreal and illusory. Whatever does not come within the range of man, whatever does not touch or modify human life in any way, is as if it were non-existent, and does not concern us one way or another. But whatever does come within our range, whatever does touch us, whatever modifies our lives in any way or to any degree, this,—whether it is physical or mental or spiritual,—by the very fact that it touches us and so concerns us, is proved to be within our reach. For, were it not within our reach, it would not touch or concern us. Since, therefore, it does touch us,—and is therefore shown to be within our reach,—we can observe it, test it, and verify it. No matter whether the observation be with the physical, the mental, or the spiritual eye, if it is reality, and we do really discern it, then this discerning is only another name for observation, the first step in the scientific method.

All reality, then, all that touches and so concerns man, —whether on earth or in the heavens above or in the depths beneath, whether it be memories or records of the past or fears or hopes of the future,—all reality is within the scope of the scientific method; and whatever can be known about it can be known in this way, and only in this way. For until that which claims to be true is verified by fresh observation and experiment, while it may or may not be true, it is only belief or opinion: it cannot be knowledge.

Since, therefore, the scientific method is the only method of knowledge, Religion must adopt it and make it her own before she can make theology—what it some day will be—the science of sciences. In that day, Religion will be the queen of the world, and Science will be her prime minister.

It has been needful for us to take so much time in clearing up the misconceptions concerning Science and its relation to religious knowledge. But since Religion is the dominant reality of human life, and therefore cannot be harmed, but only helped, by the fullest light and knowledge, we shall find it true that Science has been helping Religion all along. Her services are not all in the future: some of the grandest of them are in the past. While the mistrustful advocates of Religion have been looking askance at Science, and mistaking it for an enemy, this unrecognized knight, "with the strange device" on his shield, has entered the lists, and unhorsed a multitude of the foes of God and man. And, as his visor is lifted, we look upon the face of a champion whose countenance gleams with God's light, and whose arm wields the weapons of eternal truth, forged in the very workshops of the Almighty.

In justification of this position, I propose now to call your attention to some items of

THE DEBT OF RELIGION TO SCIENCE.

1. Science has revealed to us a universe fit to be the garment of an infinite God.

However crude their thought, men have always had some sort of notion of the world about them, of the gods or god residing in and controlling the heavens and the earth; they have had some notion of their own natures, and of the relation in which they stood to these external and superior powers. And their theology has always been their theory of these relations. All religions, then, root themselves in, spring out of, and are shaped by some cosmology, or theory of things. And the religion can be no grander or more worthy than the cosmology. A grand religion, then, must be housed in a grand conception of the universe. For an infinite God there must be an infinite home.

I need not describe in detail the childish conceptions which the childhood world entertained concerning its dwelling-place; for you are familiar with them. They were the natural fancies of barbaric people. A little flat world, with as many fancied centres as there were nations, with a limited heaven close by, the home of its peculiar gods: it is only fanciful variations of the same general plan.

The heaven and earth of Hebrew tradition, which after-ages consecrated as part of a supposed divine revelation, was shaped almost precisely after the pattern of a modern Saratoga trunk. The surface of the earth was its floor; and the sun, moon, and stars were attached to the underside of a concave dome, which would answer to the cover. Beyond it on all sides was the primeval chaos. Heaven, the home of God and His angels, was above the dome. The Church added to this conception a cavernous hell beneath,—a sort of false bottom for this trunk,—and thus completed the structure of the universe as it was popularly held, down even to mediæval times.

The Ptolemaic astronomers imagined all sorts of clumsy contrivances in their vain attempts to account for the movements of the heavenly bodies. Their sky dome was

> "With centric and eccentric scribbled o'er,
> Cycle and epicycle, orb in orb."

But so unsatisfactory was the arrangement, after all, that the acutest human intellects came to regard it as altogether unworthy of a divine contriver. Prince Alphonso of Castile said that, had he been present at the creation, he could have suggested a much better plan.

Thus, Religion not only labored under the burden of such clumsy contrivances, but her official representatives fought bitterly, and for ages, against a nobler and more worthy conception. But, against all opposition, Science persisted; and, at last, the walls of space gave way, the solid dome became the boundless expanse of air, the earth was seen "dancing about the sun," and our solar system took its place as one in the ordered maze of countless galaxies of worlds.

At last, then, we have a universe-house large enough for a God, the outlines of a temple fit to be the seat of a worship to match the boundless aspirations of the human soul. And this, in every part, is the work of Science. And Science has achieved it, not only in spite of instituted and official Religion, but for the sake of Religion; that is, Science has given to Religion a temple, one "that hath foundations, whose builder and maker is God."

2. But not only has Science revealed to Religion an

infinite universe: it has established beyond question the fact that it *is* a *universe*. It is not a chaos, but an orderly *unity*.

With the old conception of the universe, it was easy enough to believe in two gods or a thousand. No system, no unity, was discovered; and the Titanic forces seemed to be in everlasting conflict. Light fought the darkness, summer contended with winter; while cloud, wind, lightning,—all appeared to be the gigantic play of separate or hostile powers. Religion gave in her adhesion to some one deity, but was never quite sure but that the object of her worship might be some day dethroned, as Jupiter dethroned Saturn, by some other supernal king.

But, when Newton demonstrated the law of gravitation, the universe, from dust-grain to Sirius, was seen to be held in the grasp of one almighty power. Then came the proof that all the different forces of the universe were only different manifestations of one eternal force that never was less or more. And, at last, the spectroscope has revealed the wondrous fact that the dust beneath our feet is of the same material as that of which the glittering suns are made.

It is, indeed, true that Religion declared, ages ago, "The Lord our God is one Lord!" But, all the same, a hundred other religions had their "gods many and lords many;" and no one was able to do more than assert the nothingness of all but one. But, at last, science has demonstrated

"One law, one element,"

and has made it reasonable for us to complete the line, and make it read,—

"One *God*, one law, one element."

It is one force everywhere; and, if God be at all, He is now known to be only One.

And this result of knowledge is the magnificent gift to Religion of Science. The glory belongs to Science, and to Science alone.

3. Not only is the infinite oneness demonstrated, but, as already hinted,—though I wish to set the point apart, and mark it off by itself,—an infinite order is also revealed; and so we find it rational to believe in an infinite wisdom.

Of course, it is but a small part of the universe that has been explored; and even that can be said to be but partially known. But every step so far taken reveals an intelligible order. And, since our judgments are based upon experience, and each new experience reaffirms and deepens the one impression, the conviction is a cumulative one. All the known, then, being orderly, we feel an unshaken confidence that whatever seems chaotic or unwise bears that appearance to us only because it is not better known.

Here, again, as in regard to the oneness, though the religious heart might trust and hope, it is only Science that has bestowed upon Religion the power to demonstrate her magnificent faith.

4. And, once more, this order that Science has revealed is not a fixed and finished order, so that we may not hope for anything better than that which is already seen. It is rather evolution, an orderly progress, the apparent on-reaching of a purpose; and so it becomes rational for us to cherish any grandest hope as being within the scope of possibility.

Against the old universe, as a fixed and finished piece of mechanism, wrought by the hand of a supernatural contriver, certain very grave and insuperable objections could be brought. It seems to me that, on that theory, the serious criticisms of John Stuart Mill, for example, cannot be met. The God of this universe,—regarding it as a finality,—Mr. Mill thinks, cannot be both perfectly good and perfectly powerful at the same time. Either He does not wish to make things better—and, in that case, is not completely benevolent—or else He cannot make them better; and so either His wisdom or His power is impeached.

But the fact of evolution, the establishment of which is unspeakably the grandest of all the achievements of Science, completely flanks this whole class of objections, and so gives to Religion a firm basis for her noblest trust. Since all things are in process, reaching forth toward some result as yet but dimly seen, it were as illogical to condemn them for present imperfections as it would be to judge the quality of an apple that ripens only in October by tasting its puckery bitterness in July. Such judgment is as unscientific as it is irreligious. We are, then, scientifically justified in singing one verse, at least, of the old hymn of Cowper,—

> "His purposes will ripen fast,
> Unfolding every hour:
> The bud may have a bitter taste,
> But sweet will be the flower."

And, though the old watch-maker type of design may be discredited, a broader, grander, farther-reaching teleology is revealed. Taking in the wider sweep of things;

considering the growth of a system from star-dust to planet; noting the upward trend of life from protozoon to man, and, within the human range, from animal to soul; seeing how,

> "Striving to be man, the worm
> Mounts through all the spires of form,"—

in this larger survey, we are taking no unjustifiable liberty with the facts when we chant our trust in the words of Tennyson,—

> "Yet I doubt not through the ages one increasing purpose runs."

Within this generation, then, for the first time in the history of the world, Religion is able to feel beneath the feet of her faith in "the eternal goodness" the firm ground of demonstration. And this is the gift of Science.

5. Still another gift of Science to Religion is nothing less than what is essentially a spiritualist conception of the universe. There is a sort of grim irony in the fact that, while Religion has always been stigmatizing Science as materialistic, she herself has never been able to demonstrate the opposite of materialism, and has had to wait for Science to do it for her. For it is Science, at last, that has dealt materialism its death-blow, and made it reasonable for us to believe that the world is only the bright and changing garment of the living God. Religion has disbelieved and denounced materialism for ages; but, all the while, she has been haunted by it, as by a ghost which all her conjurations could not lay. But Science has now demonstrated its utter incompetence as a theory for the explanation of the universe. A theory is accepted

as valid by as much as it can account for the facts. The most important, the crucial fact with which we have to deal is conscious thought; and, in the face of this, materialism has utterly broken down. On this point, I wish to let the great voices of the scientific world be heard for themselves.

In his address on Scientific Materialism ("Fragments of Science," p. 120), Mr. Tyndall expresses the opinion that the materialist has a right to assert an intimate relation between thought and certain molecular motions in the brain. Then he adds: "I do not think he is entitled to say that his molecular groupings and his molecular motions *explain* everything. In reality, they explain nothing. . . . The problem of the connection of body and soul is as insoluble in its modern form as it was in the pre-scientific ages."

Mr. Huxley, in treating of Bishop Berkeley on the Metaphysics of Sensation ("Critiques and Addresses," p. 314), declares, "If I were obliged to choose between absolute materialism and absolute idealism, I should feel compelled to accept the latter alternative."

Instead of quoting long passages on this point from Mr. Spencer, I choose rather to give Mr. Fiske's summing up of his general position. He says, "Mr. Spencer has most conclusively demonstrated that, from the scientific point of view, the hypothesis of the materialists is not only as untenable to-day as it ever has been, but must always remain inferior in philosophic value to the opposing spiritualistic hypothesis" ("Cosmic Philosophy," vol. ii. p. 436).

And his own position Mr. Fiske sums up in these brief words: "Henceforth, we may regard materialism as ruled out, and relegated to that limbo of crudities to which we, some time since, consigned the hypothesis of special creations" ("Cosmic Philosophy," vol. ii. p. 445).

It is no part of my purpose to trace the processes of scientific reasoning by which this end has been attained. I only wish to note the fact, and to help honest religious thinkers to see and be grateful for the gifts of Science. Materialism, then, is gone by. Henceforth, Religion may gladly look upon all the fair, the magnificent, the terrible forms of matter as only veils that, while they conceal, do still more reveal the features, the outlines, and the movements of the Infinite Life that they only clothe and manifest.

6. As Science holds us by the hand, I think I may safely say that she leads us one step further into the heart of this grand mystery.

The form behind and manifested in and through what we call matter is really spirit, we say. But that is not enough for Religion. To be—in the words of Spencer—"ever in presence of an Infinite and Eternal Energy, from which all things proceed," this is grand and wonderful. But Religion has dared to hope that this infinite power was Father and Friend. And now, if Herbert Spencer may be allowed to speak for her, Science asserts, at least, demonstrable kinship between the human soul and this "Infinite and Eternal Energy." These are Mr. Spencer's words: "The final outcome of that speculation commenced by the primitive man is that the Power manifested throughout the universe distinguished as material is the same power which in ourselves wells up under the form of consciousness" (Religion: A Retrospect and Prospect).

And, with more elaboration and in greater detail, the Rev. F. E. Abbot ("Scientific Theism," p. 209) asserts of the universe, as the direct teaching and final result of science, that, "because, as an infinite organism, it thus manifests infinite Wisdom, Power, and Goodness, or thought, feeling, and will in their infinite fulness, and because these three constitute the essential manifestations of personality, it"—the universe—"must be conceived as Infinite Person, Absolute Spirit, Creative Source, and Eternal Home of the derivative finite personalities which depend upon it, but are no less real than itself.

Thus have the patient feet of Science led the way to the heights,

> ". . . through nature up to nature's God."

Such and so magnificent are her gifts to Religion.

7. But the catalogue of her services is not yet ended. Still the work goes on. For it is her spirit and method that are scattering the clouds of superstition and inhuman theology, the still lingering remnants of the primeval darkness that once overhung the whole earth, so helping Religion to break, like a sun, through the noxious vapors, and illumine the world.

Those who are committed to the impossible task of identifying with Religion dogmas and customs that cannot bear the light may well be jealous of Science and her work. For just so certainly as she is of the race of the immortals, so certainly they must die. It is the old battle between Apollo and the dragons; and the issue is not uncertain. But it is for us, as Unitarians, to accept without reserve the method of Science, which is the only method of knowledge. Then, though in ever so hopeless a minority to-day, our leadership of the world's religious future is assured. Science can destroy only God's enemies and ours; for she is the very leader of the divine armies of light and truth.

8. One more point I wish to set down, not as an achievement, but as a hope, if not a prophecy. I dare to believe that some day this same Science will discover immortality. However firmly we may believe, we cannot yet say we know. I am aware that many have no question, and say they care for no more proof. But, when any man says, "I know," the utmost that he can honestly mean is that he feels a very strong assurance. I, too, believe,—

> "I cannot think the world shall end in naught,
> That the abyss shall be the grave of thought,—
>
> That e'er oblivion's shoreless sea shall roll
> O'er love and wonder and the lifeless soul."

Neither have I any prying curiosity as to the details of that other life. But, in regard to the simple fact, I should like to feel beneath my feet the solid rock of demonstration. For could we not all bear with bravery and patience the incidents of a journey that leads to such an issue?

Now, if this other life be a fact, and if its realities be not far away, if its activities press close upon us and mingle themselves with our daily lives, I see nothing unreasonable in supposing that one day this may be demonstrated to the satisfaction of all candid men. Such, at least, is my hope.

These, then, are some items in the debt of Religion to Science. Religion is man's search after right relations to God and to his fellow-man. Science, distrusted so long, is found to be the unfallen Lucifer, the light-bearer, God's very archangel, come to guide Religion into the discovery of these relations. Let them hereafter work hand in hand in completing the foundations and rearing the homes and temples of the city of God, which is the city of a perfected humanity.

THE CHURCH IN ITS RELATION TO PUBLIC CHARITY

BY REV. EDWARD E. HALE, D.D.
OF BOSTON, MASSACHUSETTS

THE army of America is sometimes spoken of as if it were only the twenty odd thousand men, who are at the moment leading secluded and uneventful lives in certain garrisons on the sea-board or frontier posts at the West.

But the real army of America consists of every man of fighting age in the country. Of these men, the names are enrolled somewhere,—and in an exigency there are methods and forces, which array them all against the enemies of America.

It seemed a little rhetorical, a little like fustian, to say this thirty years ago. But the war demonstrated its absolute truth, as a central fact, with very terrible precision.

In precisely the same way the Church of America is sometimes spoken of as if it were one or another body of people, knit together by a certain uniform, acting under a certain discipline, who have indeed quartered themselves in certain out-of-the-way places, or among certain theories or opinions, which are unknown or unheard of in the active world. But the real Church of America consists of every man, woman, and child who has been born among the Christian influences of Christian Law and Christian Society. So far as these people do wrong—intentionally and by system—they belong to Satan and his company. But the same individuals, so far as they attempt the right, and do the right, belong to the Church of Christ. They cannot help themselves. The Christian ichor found its way into their veins when they first drew breath. Christian blankets warmed them in their babyhood. Christian law protected them. Christian wheat and Christian milk fed them. Christian schools taught them. They live in a social order which Christ founded. And precisely as they are Americans because they are born in America, or because they have chosen to live here, precisely so they are, in a broad and in a true sense, members of a Christian Society. When the Church needs help, she sounds her trumpet-call. "The Spirit and the bride say come." And they come to do her work, without uniform, without discipline, if you please, but all the same, they come.

It is necessary to make this fundamental distinction in the beginning of a statement on the work of the Church in charity. For we are told, quite too often, both by friends and enemies, that the great public charities are not in the hands of the Church in America, but that they are in the hands of another body, which is called the State. And, in the same spirit, almost every sophomore who speaks for a college prize, and every school-girl who reads a dissertation on graduation, tells us that in America the Church and the State are absolutely separated, and that it is very fortunate that it is so. But the truth is that there never was a State so permeated and enlivened by distinctly religious influences as the State is with us. It is true that the five hundred little separate ecclesiastical organizations are compelled, as organizations, to keep their hands off the ark of the State. Woe to any Uzzah of them all who forgets that, and puts its hand out to handle it. Be the offender the nineteenth secession from the Reformed Covenanters, or be it the Church of Rome,—which seceded from the historical Church some twelve centuries ago,—the ark as it moves on will crush it to powder. But, all the same, the infinite sway of absolute Religion,—the realities of Faith, Hope, and Love, will govern public conduct, real statesmanship, and all local and all national law. How can it be otherwise? The man votes for Representative or President to-day, who voted yesterday in Synod, Conference, or Assembly. The man teaches here who teaches there. The leaders in the one enterprise are, by the very law of leadership, the leaders in the other. And so, step by step, the objects which the Church has at heart, in Faith, in Hope, and in Love, are taken up and carried out by the organization which we call the State. It is thus, and thus only, that by a perfectly simple advance, the State has assumed the direction of Public Charity and of Public Education. In both these matters the Church has always known that she had important duties. And never has she acted more wisely than in compelling the State to take many of the details of them in hand. Witness the contrast between the thorough way in which both these matters are taken in hand,—say in

Philadelphia, or in New York,—compared with the slip-shod way in which they are left dragging by the ecclesiastical authorities in such a city as Rome.

So far as the business of the Church Universal goes, in that wider definition of the Church which includes all children of God so far as they try to do His will in a Christian land, little need be said here. It is enough to say, that every member of that great unembodied body must keep the highest and noblest Ideal in view before the State, and must be satisfied with nothing less. Has the State to establish institutions for the blind, she asks at once, "How many blind people are there who need this instruction? We will have no favoritism, no selection of candidates; we will educate all who come or none." This magnificent inclusion of all the sons of God is more than princely. It is democratic. I have not observed that princes do such things. But precisely as princes have taught us that you can build prisons large enough for all, we must teach the State that she can build hospitals, schools, asylums, and other infirmaries large enough for all. We will not let her fall into the mistake of supposing that an Institution, because it is an Institution, is respectable. That is mediæval. But the State shall not count the cost in any niggardly way. The State shall understand that one child of God is as good as another. And this great lesson the Church must teach to her. And there must be no convict diet at this feast at which the State sits at the head of the table. The education which the State offers must give the beggar's child the chance, which the prince would have, born in the purple. Who knows whether it is in hovel or in palace that the next Shakespeare or the next Beethoven is to be born? Neither Church nor State can afford to neglect him when he comes.

Not simply in holding up this high ideal, but in a hundred details of special and local duty, it will be the business of a separate church or congregation to work out problems yet new, and attend to details which no other organization can handle. It is specially to consider this duty that I am here,—and it is only by way of caution that I have alluded to that Largest Office which the Church has in hand. There will always be, thank God, a disposition among eager Christian men and women to form societies for the relief of human suffering and sorrow in its several forms. We want, very naturally, to attack separate enemies. In a highly organized community, say such a community as this, there will be a Society to protect Children, a Prison Society, a Hospital for Consumptives, a Society of St. George, and so on, caring for this and that detail of human need,—and caring some well,—some poorly,—some wholly and some by halves. Each of these societies may receive or reject its subjects. The blind institution may reject a deaf man. The deaf and dumb institution may reject a blind man. St. George's Society may reject an Irishman. St. Patrick's may reject an Englishman. But there is one Society,—and its name is the Church of Christ,—which must reject nobody who comes within its territory. That territory may be large or small. But within its lines the Church must never say no. It never admits the impossible, because it has infinite resources.

They asked President Wayland once if the Unitarian Church was a Christian Church. "Can it pass the test?" he said, "Can it cast out the devils?" The answer was the true answer. The Church of Christ professes that it can do what he did, and even that it can do greater things than these. When, therefore, a hospital rejects a patient, because the case is chronic,—or an asylum a child, because the institution is full,—or a Lodge a widow, because her husband had not paid his assessments,—this rejected husk, which is not fine enough to pass through the bolting-cloth, applies to the Church of Christ, and the Church is bound by the law of its being to see that the right thing is done. It has no right to say that the worst drunkard is irreclaimable. For it affects to be the representative and agent of Him whose precise business it is to save the world from its sins.

I. It will generally be found convenient, and probably necessary, for each church to define, in advance, its territorial range, and not to scatter its forces by pretending to assume every duty. For a church, as for a man, it is better, it is best, to do thoroughly what it does at all. And, in city life, a church will find it easy to assume for itself a certain specific district, where its different agents shall come to be known and shall feel at home; where, as the commonplace says, they can make one hand wash another. What you want is, that all parties in that region shall know this specific church, as really, and in good faith, representing the benevolence and the activity of the good God. I do not believe that it takes a long time for a church, which is in earnest, to win for itself this reputation. If there are four hundred churches in a city of a million people,—each one of them, on the average, might take thus the oversight of twenty-five hundred people;—say, as we live, of three hundred and fifty separate homes. Suppose an accredited agent looked in regularly at the Criminal Court, and repeated at the church office the names of the people sent to the House of Correction from the two or three blocks which the church had in hand. Suppose an immediate inquiry in each family, from which the bread-earner had been carried to prison; or, in the case of a bad boy or girl, suppose immediate effort made for the provision of a better home, of other training, or some chance for reform. Let the church have at its disposal a friendly nurse, who, in any case of sickness among these three hundred and fifty families, shall look in with kindly succor and sympathy, shall teach the young mother how to wash and dress her baby, shall find for the children some vent or outlet for their noise and energy, while the mother lies sick and faint; shall bring in order for chaos, and sweetness for filth. Suppose such a nurse, or some watchful coterie of advisers, knows who are the helpful people of the neighborhood,—who will watch with a sick man where there is need,—will supply motherhood, where the mother is disabled; who, with or without compensation or honorarium, will bring in the miracles of personal and affectionate care. Suppose every boy of the three hundred and fifty families is invited to the pretty and cheerful reading-room of the chapel by a light in the window, or a ticket in his pocket. Suppose there is a magic lantern there Tuesday, and a debating club Friday,—and the street boy finds he is made welcome,—and indeed that he is somebody:—finds that a game of checkers or the "Swiss Family Robinson" is, on the whole, better fun than swearing at his mates, or running to fires. Suppose, even, that the man who last month paid for his coal three times its market cost because he bought by the basket, finds that because he is in this district, he may take it at the coal-depot for the price which gentlemen pay who take it by the ton. Such timid approach to Communism may be excused in the machinery of a church, whose first members, while they believed in separate property, never said much about it. It is written of them that "no man said these things were his own." They did not talk about them, because they held each man his gifts in trust for all.

That church is fortunate which is itself anywhere in or near the district to which it thus ministers. The church building itself, the regular and the occasional services may be made a great help in what is done for the higher life of the region. A church so fortunate as this in which we are—with rooms for any form of hospitality—would have a great advantage if within half a mile of its chapel it could select a region on which it should, so to speak, try its experiments of education, of charity, of public amusement,—or, speaking more generally, of Religion or of Life.

II. I have spoken thus in detail, of concentration of power gained by the work of one church in one district,—because I think any vagueness as to the work of *the* Church in charity comes from the indefiniteness with which such work is sometimes attempted. The churches have been fired with a noble enthusiasm for foreign missions; the enthusiasm has been none too large, the amounts expended have been, after all, too small,— and the results have been magnificent. In that business, from the nature of the case, almost, the work has to be done largely by the contribution of money; money has to be paid into a common treasury, and it is impossible to say where any single church is acting. One dollar of its contribution is spent in Paris, and another perhaps in the Caroline Islands. No one would complain of this. But all the more does that church need to take in hand some definite work at home, of which the results can be closely studied,—and which may call not for the money only, but for the real life and hearty personal effort of those involved. In the case I have supposed,—if in the city in question the charities were generally organized on what we call the Chalmers plan, or the Elberfeld plan,—it would gradually come about that in the selected district this church named many, perhaps most of the friendly visitors. In the end the church would be proud of its success,—and would have bridged for that region the gulf, which in city life is so apt to separate prosperity from shiftlessness.

III. It is, yet again, the duty of a church organization to lead the public attention to new lines of charity work, where, perhaps, some experiments may be needed, or where the public mind may not yet be prepared for the use of the public funds.

The same thing can be done, of course, and well done, by a specialist society, made on purpose. But there is, perhaps, extra friction, extra expense, extra care. The members of one church, on the other hand, know each other, are often together,—they have an established office and treasury, with the other facilities of organization. They can try an experiment and drop it if it fails. And, above all, they need employ no salaried or professional philanthropists. They will not work on a very large scale without organizing the independent special society. But Dr. Wollaston and many of the physicists have taught us that some experiments are best tried on a small scale.

The teaching of sewing in the public schools is a successful instance of such experiments. And, in Philadelphia, I can speak of this experiment as a matter of history, where the business has gone through all its grades. What more natural than that a spirited woman, determined to make people better,—that is, more fit to do the duty next their hands,—should call half a dozen or a dozen girls into her house, or into the church vestry, on their half holiday, and should teach them to sew. How certain that the hard-pressed mothers who hear of it shall send their children! How certain that on her side she shall enlist assistants, easily found among that large class of girls who want to be of use somewhere, but dare not volunteer into the Sunday-school! They can, at least, thread a needle, or tie a knot in a thread, or read a story. Your school is formed; it succeeds; it outgrows its quarters. Other schools are formed in the same way. And at last supervisors, and school-committee men, and other people in authority find that the thing is popular and will go, and they give you, rather grudgingly at first, the use of the public school-rooms, a reasonable bit of school time, and the advantages of enforced discipline. In the end they pay the salary of the teacher. You find that your pretty vestry work is taken off your hands. But you do not sorrow for that, when you know that thirty thousand girls are receiving the benefit which you planned for thirty. I may say in passing that in my own city we are passing through the second stage of this process in the matter of schools for cooking. The pioneers seem to have solved the necessary questions. They seem to have found out good ways of teaching and of discipline. They have found out how much time is needed and when it is best used. I am assured by an expert that an intelligent girl of fourteen, at the end of a year's course of two lessons a week, is well up in all the essentials of the business of cooking. The girls themselves delight in the training, and consider it a great privilege to attend. What I call the second stage is this: the city gives the use of the school building. The private charity supplies the machinery and material and pays the teachers. The public authorities detail the scholars, on an average, thirty from each girls' school in the favored districts. The precise number under such public instruction in Boston annually, is now three hundred and sixty.

I have mentioned these two illustrations, not from their special intrinsic importance, but as convenient instances which show how a work undertaken on a small experimental scale may grow, if it ought to grow, and so enlarge itself as to prove its utility, and indeed compel the well-knit organization of taxpayers or officials, which we call the State, to adopt its plans and carry them forward. When the State is ready, the officers of any church may well give their ready assent to such a transfer. They will have no pride in keeping their infant in their hands, when he has grown large enough to be safe in the care of the Public. They will always be able to find opportunities for the use of all the energy, and money, and ingenuity which they have at command.

IV. There is one element of Force which any church can use,—better, perhaps, than any other of an existing organization,—and that is the willingness of young people to be of service also.

I think it will be recognized as a general experience by all persons interested in Sunday-schools, that by the time boys are fourteen or fifteen years old they begin to be restless about Sunday-school attendance. They would say, if they said anything, that it was "babyish" or "goodyish." Or they would say that they did not care for catechism work any longer. At an age rather more advanced, something of the same protest comes from girls, though not so certainly. The truth is these boys and girls begin to feel that they are going to be men and women, and that they have some of the responsibilities of manhood and womanhood. In all this they are quite right, and that church is wise that takes them at their word and gives them some sphere for real useful activity.

The experience of which I have been asked to speak of the various clubs which call themselves "Wadsworth Clubs," or "Look Up Legions," or "Ten Times One Clubs," runs in these lines. They are organizations now of four young people, now of four hundred, now of boys, now of girls, now of both sexes together. Under whatever form, they are bound to do distinct work for the benefit of others as a part of their purpose in organizing. And this should not be merely superficial work. It should not be the peddling of tickets for a church fair. These boys and girls should see that they practically and really touch the work of the world. Let their organization be a way of showing them how other people live. The experiences of these clubs, as they have themselves published them, show how boys and girls can be interested in the work of hospitals, in the care of the sick, in the welcome of exiles, in the education of others who deserve more than they are likely to get, and they show as well that this interest is no matter of baby talk, but that it may result in a very considerable working power. There has been so much of this experience, that the reports of its failures and successes will be of a good deal of value to any church which wishes to utilize so large an element of power.* In almost every one of the directions of the activity of the church in cities to which I have alluded, the alliance of such an organization of the young people will prove of value,—as in the establishment of a reading-room in the neighborhood, as in the friendly visits of a friendly nurse, or in reading to the blind or to the sick. Such things, when you begin with boys or girls of fourteen years of age, may seem to amount to very little; but time soon passes, and when ten years have gone by, the special church which has tried the experiment and the community which it has tried to serve, knows what it is to have such a body of men and women, who understand by the practical experience which ten years have given them, how the rich can help the poor, how the wise can serve the unwise, how and where the native citizen, used to the position, can help the stranger. Both as an active force for to-day and as an education for the better activities of the future, such clubs have already proved their value.

I will not detain you longer. I have not tried to disguise the truth that in our communities the work of

---

* These Reports have been published by J. S. Smith & Co., Boston.

the church in charity will often be only tentative. It is our business to try experiments, and when they have succeeded to pass them over to that organization which we call the State. It will seem sometimes, therefore, as if what we do were petty. Small it may be, but it is not petty. It is not insignificant. We ought to be glad and proud to lead the way, and quite willing when we have succeeded to transfer to others both the credit and the responsibility. Certain things there are which a church can always do for its neighborhood better than any other organization can do it. It should be so quick and its organization so elastic that it can do these things. It can certainly be a light to those who are around it. It can certainly offer companionship to those that are alone. It can offer encouragement to those who are disheartened. It can give vantage and a starting-point for those who do not know how to begin.

THE CHURCH AS A SCHOOL OF ETHICS

BY REV. THOMAS R. SLICER

OF PROVIDENCE, RHODE ISLAND

THE President of Harvard College has said more than once lately that no method had been yet discovered by which morality can be taught without religion. This too sweeping statement is the negative expression for the inquiry intended as the theme of this essay, which in more positive phrase would stand, "How can Religion become the introduction to Morality?" For whether it be conceded or not conceded that this is the true order of importance, still, it is the order of fact and of nature. Religion was in the world as a concrete expression of man's nature before any system of ethics expressed the terms on which he should order his conduct. And naturally so, for in some form the individual takes account of himself before he accounts for his fellows; and it is only reasonable from the stand-point of the primitive man that he shall be able rather to propitiate the powers he fears, than that he should settle the terms on which he should live with the human beings he does not fear and may not yet wholly love. For the unseen powers have him at a disadvantage and it his business to know their will,—but the forces, like his own, about him, human passions and powers—well, if he cannot live with them, he will live in spite of them. That this order is now reversed is due to two influences, one of reaction,—a reaction made up of many elements; the other the difficulty of settling the terms on which we shall maintain ethical relations with our fellows,—for a growing civilization means, and ascending reason and reason in the ascendant mean, the multiplication of defences as well as the increasing variety of human wants and opportunities of mutual help. We will consider now the first cause which has given morality, temporarily at least, the first place in importance.

It is not simply that having passed through the first table of the Law we have reached the second table. For those who elevate ethics to the first place do not say as did Jesus of Nazareth, "This is the first commandment, Thou shalt love the Lord thy God with all thy heart and soul and strength; and the second *is like unto it:* Thou shalt love thy neighbor as thyself!" They do not recognize the wisdom here contained, that there may be a first and a second commandment, but there can be no great and little commandment. They are disposed to accept the question which is the greatest commandment of the Law on the ground there implied and to answer, Right human relations constitute the chief study of man. "Conduct is three-fourths of life." "Whoever is shipwrecked in this life is shipwrecked on conduct." Religion is morality grown imaginative, allowing itself a flowering out at the capital, knowing that it is the column's upright lines that support the weight of responsibility.

So that for this forging of ethics to the front there must be given some better reason than that its time has come in the course of human development. It is the product of reaction, and the insistence of its advocates is in the exact ratio in which this previous restraint has been felt.

No discussion of the subject under treatment, The Church as a School of Ethics, could be at all entered upon without taking account first of the Church as *an immoral influence* in civilization.

The appeal to history reveals the Church as grounded upon the idea of an elect people,—to whom has been made a special revelation,—by means of a supernatural interference with the genesis of human life, by virtue of which the "all power given" to its hands is perpetuated in hands specially selected to do as a College of Apostles the work, a pattern of which had been given as an impossible ideal to be imitated as far as may be. Of course there must centre here secret services, to which admittance is gained by a knowledge of some pass-word, or by the purchase of some favorable consideration by virtue of which mysteries known to a few are imparted to a few more. So that the "caste and class" idea derived from a people whose spiritual progenitor was the friend of God, was perpetuated as a slowly enlarging class by initiation. In other words, the narrow spirit of Judaism was married to the narrow practice of heathenism; and though this union was brooded by the wide-winged spirit of Greek Philosophy, it was a union sterile and capable only of adopting as children forms of service and methods of worship which it had not the power to infuse with its own life. Institutions last longer than ideas,—as ruined sanctuaries are witnesses that the God worshipped there has been forgotten, and his worshippers are dead. But the ruins remain. They may be beautified with vines and may shelter the wild creatures of the night, but the æsthetic admirer by day and the flitting bat by night see in them no moral significance.

In this there is found the first reason for a moral reaction against the Church of history; that it has not set to work to adjust human relations as its founder did, but has sought to adjust human beings in right relations to itself.

A second contribution to this reaction may be found in that immoral influence, which was contributed by the chief doctrine of this Church of history, namely, the shifting of moral obligation from the lives of men to the altars of sacrifice. I do not need to rehearse the varied phases in which this idea of a changed emphasis as to life sought to lift the inconvenient stress of life. Whether known as "imputed righteousness" or as imparted absolution, the Church taught men under many immoral aspects the heresy to human life that God was concerned with His own character at the sacrifice of man's. The Church for sixteen hundred years insisted upon the fact that righteousness was one thing in God and a wholly different thing in man, and dominated human life by an imperial command rather than by an imperative ideal.

The gain by slow degrees of reason's strength, in spite of the effort to carry on human relations by the monarchical method of the Church, discovered the fallacy of the Church's teaching, and for a little while—that is, a little while by comparison with the time of restraint—there threatened a reaction in the form of a blind materialism. "Men," as Turgot has said, "watched nature, and as their eyes wandered over the surface of the profound ocean, instead of the bed hidden under the waters, they saw nothing but the reflection of their own faces." But even this was better than "imputed righteousness," which was what has been aptly called "a forged note to meet a fictitious debt." Fontanelle expresses the result in the statement, "God made man in His own image, but then man returns the favor by making God in his."

A single quotation must suffice to show this: "As the Sun when he riseth obscureth, and darkeneth the light of the skies and dismisseth and scattereth them: even so the righteousness of faith, which for Christ's sake is imputed unto us, doth vanquish the darkness and driveth away the night of the glory of men's works."

It is not a pleasure to refer to this historical antagonism between the human sense of rectitude and what the Church has taught as the divine scheme of salvation. But it seems necessary, as briefly displaying the ground for the feeling so much insisted upon that the Church cannot become "a School of Ethics." One other cause of reaction is involved in the foregoing: The declamations of the pulpit and the arguments of Christian advocates against what they call "the filthy rags of human righteousness." This distinction between Divine Grace and human gracelessness proceeded to its logical conclusion when it was said that "Jesus Christ put over the sackcloth of our humanity the cloth-of-gold of his divinity." The idea could take no more repellant form to express how entirely we were by nature the children of wrath, and how impossible it was for any works of righteousness which we could do to meet recognition upon the part of God. No wonder, therefore, from all these causes operating in a multitude of ways through diverse channels, there grew up the sense of the need of a system of ethics wholly separated from the Church.

This Revolution was a Holy War. The men it produced made independent thought possible; the interregnum it threatened was occupied by heroic advance guards, who held the heights until the main body could be brought forward. The atheism of reaction went into the fields and woods, into the laboratory and the dissecting-room, and confessed at length, "Whither shall I go from thy Spirit, and whither shall I flee from thy Presence?—thou art above Heaven, thou art beneath the nether world. The outmost boundaries are as inner lines to thy wider horizon, whither the wings of the morning bear me,—thou art everywhere; the darkness, even my darkness, hideth not from thee. The darkness and the light are both alike to thee. Thou hast beset me behind and before, and laid thy hand upon me!"

The Church was discovered as not essential to the Idea of God. The Idea of God was the essential of the idea of the universe.

We are accustomed to read that figure of the New Testament about the new wine and the new bottles, as though having the new wine we must order the new bottles forthwith. Such an interpretation overlooks that power of correspondence between the secular meaning of terms and the divine idea they are used to convey. We do the world scant justice for its power of suggestion. It is doubtless true that each season brings its new wine, for each season brings from the fruitful earth its ripe grapes,—but the new wine is not in the grapeskin, nor yet does it wait for the wine-skin. It is somewhere between these two while its processes go forward, by which it becomes new wine. It passes through safe conduits and is preserved in safe receptacles. So it is with the growing moral consciousness, it does not create the terms of its expression simply,—it takes also the form of that which expresses it. If the world of secular life had not risen, it had been able to set no shores to the rising religious tide. Terms change their meaning,—does "father" mean the same to us as to a Roman or a Jew? Does "wife" mean the same to us as to a Greek? Is not the *familia* something holier than when it was a group of slaves over whom the master held the power of life and death? Is not the king a different being from that creature of divine prerogatives who was "defender of the faith" and corrupter of the faithful? "The king can do no wrong,"—so went the phrase,—it is still true that the king can do no wrong because of the constitutional limits which will not permit it. The Lord's anointed must prove his anointing not by a crowned head, but by a glorified character. Even the doctrine of the Fatherhood of God has taken on a different and tenderer meaning because fatherhood itself is a different and more tender relationship. Thus it appears that a reflex action is discoverable from the secular side of life by virtue of which the meaning of terms is changed because the thing meant is changed. We need not busy ourselves about the new bottles for the new wine,—when the new wine is ready the new wine-skin will be found ready also.

The Church of History is not the Church of to-day. The charges brought against it as immoral are not in evidence as formerly. It is senseless declamation to go on charging sins upon heirs of an estate because of the mistakes of him from whom they inherit. It is like that socialistic sophism that since certain things do not belong demonstrably to somebody, they therefore ought to belong to everybody.

The Church of to-day is neither the Church of history nor a ruin left by its removal. It is a survival; it is a new birth. It is a witness to a "method of the divine Life," which has been appearing in the world in all ages. "The fulness of the time" is not the end of creative energy, but an incident in the life of God. The world's epochs are God's thoughts,—its incarnations are the articulate utterances of the Eternal Reason. The word is made flesh,—full of grace and truth, —its glory is as of the only begotten of the Father; but in this we are misled by our admiration and awe. "How precious are thy thoughts, O God. How great is the sum of them, they are more than can be numbered!" Surviving institutions are able to survive because they still share the life of God. The demand for ethical teaching is made upon the Church. The task set us is to show that *the Church is capable of ethical passion*.

Now let us come to definition,—for almost all our confusion arises from an undefined haze, from which no sharp boundary-lines yet appear. Such nebulous uncertainty meets our gaze when we try to interpret the terms Religion, Worship, Ethics.

Theology is sharply defined, but we have nothing to do with that any more in this discussion,—the censer is perfectly definite in shape, but it is not prayer. The gargoyle is a definite hideous or grotesque form, which sheds the water from the church roof by defining its course, but it is not the church. It is the infirmity of our thinking that the things defined are not the essential things. The censer swings before the altar, while the soul sits steady and watches for God. The church walls rise and its enclosure is perfect and its appointments beautiful, and all according to the plan determined beforehand; but is there any pattern shown to any lawgiver on any mount of vision by which the Church shall be formed? No! The Church is something more interior and spiritual. It exists without an edifice. The edifice is built for it, but *it* is "builded together for an habitation of God through the spirit."

The Church then has to do with God. It is *based* not upon earthly relationships. It rises as the earthly representative of an unseen Eternal Presence. Its business is with the world, but still "the souls of the sons of God are greater than their business."

Religion, which is more than the sum of all Religions, is the subjective state of which the Church is the objective fact. Let us try to define what we mean by Religion. If there were only two beings in the Universe and there had been no more than two,—God and the man,—then for one of these beings, as we conceive it, apart from all its accidents, RELIGION WOULD BE A PASSIONATE DEVOTION TO THE WILL OF GOD. Religion possesses one of these beings, the other is its object. This, for the purposes of this essay, is the sufficient definition of Religion.

Religion is a passionate devotion to the will of God.

Mark you, it is no mere sentiment satisfied by self-surrender; nor a passion for devotion, which has for its epitaph "the zeal of thy House hath consumed me." It is rather like the bush on Horeb, it burns with fire, but is not consumed; for it is not the bush that burns, but God within the bush. This, in man, is the correspondent to the thought of God. God is and man is. God "remembers that man is dust." And man has a sense of God that the dust cannot wholly extinguish. So, then, this is the beginning of a moral order; now first the Infinite will has had its signal answered. The flame has kindled a new fire, and Religion appears *as passionate devotion to the will of God.*

What is the next stage in this development? You answer "worship." Yes, it is worship, not prayer. No, that is also an incident; that is not in the essential definition. Worship is this passionate devotion to the will of God going out of itself to discover what that will appoints. It communes with God in the night watches and is still; it anticipates the dawning of the morning with its lighted countenance,—"When I awake I am still with Thee." If thou art not near, then "I trust, and wait patiently for Thee." "My soul fainteth for the longing that it hath for thy testimonies at all times." "Thy statutes have been my song in the House of my pilgrimage." Thus does this man whom God hath found, and whose devotion has become a passion, seek to know the will of God. This is worship,— all else is its incident.

Now, let us suppose that the Infinite Will has been answered in another soul, so that a passionate devotion to the will of God moves two men at once,—it moves them to a common centre in their worship; they seek not each other, but God, each going out of himself to find the Divine Will; they go at the same pace, they seek the same end, they meet in the same centre. When they meet, though they may have never looked each in the other's eyes, yet now moving from far-sundered planes of life and experience, being so met, they constitute the Church. It may be a man and woman meeting for life together on this plane of the will of God; no matter, it is then "the Church that is in thy house."

When the passionate devotion to the will of God in two souls goes forth to find in worship what that will appoints, the Church has come. The new Jerusalem has "descended out of heaven from God." What is the proof of this unity as a church? If it is a unit you cannot make it more complete. You may enlarge the number, but each added soul is taken up into the unity, existent before you have enlarged the sphere; you have not made it more a sphere, it has "that true sphericity which receives every ray of the concave Heavens." On the other hand, you cannot destroy this unit by bringing to it any uninspired soul. Such an one, without passionate devotion to the will of God, remains attached to the perfect sphere; it is no part of it. It is as foreign as the barnacle and the fungus; it can never be the Church except by assimilation, and when that time comes it is no longer attached to the spiritual sphere from the outside, but has disappeared by incorporation into the living organism, to appear henceforth as *augmented devotion to the will of God, going out of itself to seek what that will appoints.*

Am I not right in saying this is not the Church of history? Neither is it, except ideally, the Church of to-day. But it is that older and still living Church of God, which has always existed since the kindling soul of man met the kindled soul of man at that common centre, the will of God.

My declaration is that in the *Church thus realized is the proper field of ethics.*

For in this act of worship, bringing these two human souls to a common centre in God, their sense of God is succeeded by a sense of each other. Two moral beings have met upon the same plane, have moved by a common impulse to a common centre, and whether they will or no, they are in ethical relations by virtue of their being. And herein lies the defect of Dr. Martineau's definition of ethics. He declares "ethics to be the doctrine of human character." Human character in correspondence, rather, is the point where ethics begin.

Or take this other definition of the same Christian philosopher, "ethics treat of the right ordering of personal relations, so far as they may be made better or worse by our will." But personal relations precede any question of will and antedate any act of right ordering. These relations begin the moment the lives of two moral beings touch. They are not assumed, they appear at the point of contact, they result from personal qualities, they represent the correspondence between persons as distinguished from the juxtaposition of things. A moral being does not become so by intention. A man becomes an honest or a dishonest trader when he meets another who desires to purchase what he has to sell, but the question of his being honest precedes that moment, as the *man* goes before the *merchant.*

We behold in the Church thus defined the first guarantee of its efficiency as a School of Ethics, namely,—

I. The moral relation between two human beings is grounded in a common relation to a Higher Being. This is not simply saying that the will of God is a necessary standard of righteousness; for that would open the further question, what is the will of God and how determined? But the statement that a moral relation between two human beings is grounded in a common relation to a higher Being, in the Church as it has been defined, is simply declaring a security for this ethical relation in the fact that it does not vibrate between two souls, but swings them together toward a higher soul than theirs. Neither in mechanics nor in morals has the discovery yet been made how to expend power and transform the expenditure into a new supply. In mechanics, this would be "perpetual motion." But we must always allow for waste and friction, and as in mechanics so in morals, the only way to provide against these is for a reserve of power on which to draw.

In ethics no relation exists for its own sake,—two natures correspondent simply to each other will weary of that relationship. The ground of their correspondence must be outside themselves and above themselves. As the great planets are in equipoise as to each other, because they are in perfect relation to the centre of their united motion. Ethics, for the sake of ethics, grow stale, and become exhausted or mechanical. Ethics holding constant relationship to a common source of inspiration have the power of sustained action.

The man who, in this last quarter of the nineteenth century, is ashamed to start in his thinking with the idea of God, is not necessarily infidel, but he is necessarily ignorant. He has begun to fulfil the prophecy which Professor Huxley uttered twenty-one years after the publication of "The Origin of Species" by Darwin. He said, "History warns us that it is the customary fate of new truths to begin as heresies and end as superstitions, and as matters now stand it is hardly rash to anticipate that in another twenty years the new generation, educated under the influences of the present day, will be in danger of accepting the main doctrines of the origin of species with as little reflection, and it may be as little justification, as so many of our contemporaries, twenty years ago, rejected them."

Let such timid souls reassure themselves. It is no longer considered an evidence of scientific vision to declare we have looked into the heavens and they are void, that we have called and there was no answer. No man need now be ashamed to declare that the being of God lies back of all moral relationships, and that all such relationships, when they are vital, do not end in themselves; their reference is beyond themselves and above themselves. A system of ethics which exists for its own sake has in that fact the guarantee of its dissolution. Dogmatic morals are no better than dogmatic speculations. All vital organisms live from a centre and grow outward. The Church is an organism. Ethics are that organism recognizing the interdependence of the parts and the total dependence of the whole upon its source of being in God.

The Church as a School of Ethics has its further guarantee in the fact that,—

II. It owns allegiance to an IMPERATIVE IDEAL.

It had its origin in ethical passion in the soul of a man to whom the setting of men in right relations to each other grew out of the discovery of the man's right relation to God.

With the discovery of the Fatherhood of God went the conviction of the brotherhood of men. Jesus of Nazareth had no system of morals; he had no thesis to defend. He spoke of bearing witness to the truth as a man would demonstrate the fact that one line was perpendicular to another, and that the interval between their separated extremes was ninety degrees. He was not concerned about truths as statements of a system of truth. Much less was truth to him a weapon of controversy. There never was a more transparent teacher, because he was perfectly sure of his point of view and could tell what he saw. His adjustment of human relations was not for the sake of making conduct right, but to place men so they could see what he saw, and see it equally, one not obstructing the other's vision. A man without calculation, simply an obedient will dominated by an imperative Ideal.

A will that is trained to obey is not a will subjugated, but educated; sensitive to high behests, alert to fulfil the will of God. The whole nature falls into line at the command of its ideal.

Such a unifying of a man's nature is of prime importance. It is as different from all mechanical adjustments as life is different from machinery. Actions, conduct, in which the details of life are fitted carefully together, may make a mosaic which will look like a picture, but it will never be more than a mimicry of nature, in which life penetrates every part and calls it obedient to a great design. "The greatest good of the greatest number," or the highest pleasure of the individual itself the greatest good of all, may serve as a rule to work by, but it is dependent upon statistics and calculation which love spurns as it rises with direct flight whither its highest aspirations take their way.

George Macdonald says well that "duty is a ponderous roll of canvas which love spreads aloft into a tent to dwell in."

The Church as a School of Ethics to prescribe the terms of human conduct enforced as duty, would crumble under the weight of its own burden and crush its children with its fall.

But the Church is a School of Ethics because the burdens of duty are carried in the bosom of love, and love turns by its ever-present divine overshadowing the sacraments of sorrow into festivals of gladness. Of that great loving Son of God who called the Church first together it was written, "Because thou hast loved righteousness and hated iniquity, God, even thy God, hath anointed thee with the oil of gladness above thy fellows."

Human conduct maintains right relations when it finds an inspiration large enough to transfigure its sense of duty and raise service to the dignity of affection.

A passionate devotion to the will of God, kindled in souls brought together to a common centre in the service of that will, guarantees an ideal life which each will help the others lead, and in leading it each shall win delight. In this also "the joy of the Lord is your strength!"

But one must anticipate the objection sure to be advanced, that this is too ideal and lacks a recognition of the organized Church everywhere present, and which begins to doubt whether it is possible in its organization to be a School of Ethics, as it has been a School of Theology.

The answer is very simple.

It was a School of Theology, because it sought to generalize, in statements purely intellectual, the phenomena of the spiritual nature of man *as related to the idea of God*. If it is a School of Ethics, it will be because it has been able to state in the terms of moral life, leading up to conduct and speech, the phenomena it has discovered in the spiritual life of man *as related to man*. And as in theology the one abiding element is the spiritual nature of man, conscious of itself and of God; so in ethics the abiding element will be the spiritual nature of man conscious of itself and of another man. And just as a clearer view of God came at last to be confessed to be a deeper consciousness of self,—saying, "I am seeking to bring the God that is in me into harmony with the God that is in the universe;" so a clearer view of ethical relations will come back to the deeper knowledge of self,—saying, "I am seeking to bring the humanity within me into correspondence with the humanhood in the world." In each case it is the man, who has discovered the core of his being,—the man within the man, the spiritual below the psychical, as the psychical lies back of the carnal.

It is a discovery of prime importance when an enlightened child of God declares, "I have a body, but I am a spirit." This is the underlying fact both of theology and of ethics, for it provides the thought of that above the man which calls out his reverence, and that beside the man which supplies the opportunity for service.

THE CHURCH AS A SCHOOL OF ETHICS 147

If the Church be organized around that confidence in the spiritual nature of man it will be a living organism; if it is gathered as particles cohering simply by a mutual attraction, the most symmetrical organization will have the compactness of a statue, but can never have the vitality of a living man. The beauty of a statue is always pathetic and powerless. There is but one image of life more remote from the thing imaged, and that is a body out of which the life has gone. The statue mimics life, the corpse has been flung aside by life it will never be able to overtake. Such is an organized assembly of men and women who seek to get into ethical relations except by the way of life, and by life I mean spiritual being, all else is but the thing built up around life.

Let a single illustration suffice. Suppose in an organized church there be represented two classes caught in that vital struggle now going forward between labor and the employers of labor. If these classes have met for what is called with unconscious irony, "divine service," they are in ethical relations, by the fact that they are moral beings; but they ignore these relations and substitute for them antagonisms of interest. Now, when you have allowed for ignorance of the laws of trade in the laborer and for ignorance of the way men live and feel in the employer of labor, what have you still as the ground of their antagonism? Is it a want of devotion to the church? they both have an interest in it and love it. But men feel this for their club, or mill, or colleges. Is it a lack of loyalty to their religious teacher? they both hear him, and say he is an admirable man who knows nothing of the world. What is it, then, that they lack? Is it an understanding of each other? Neither can see the other, because what each stands for intercepts the sight of each. No, if they can even be brought together to calm and candid statement of their contending claims, that which will result will be a compromise effected upon the ground of expediency, it will be a healing of differences in the interests of profit and wages; in other words, in the interest of physical existence; but suppose these men should meet in the true Church, where souls moving from sundered planes of life come to one centre with passionate devotion to the will of God. Then, instead of their interests being laid side by side with cold contact, in the white-heat of that divine passion their destinies would be welded together by every stroke of disaster. What men need is not so much a prompt philanthropy, or a scheme of ethics built from hypothesis on the one hand, or experiment on the other. *They need God.* Not plans of living, but life; not remedies for disease, but health, the foe of all diseases.

When will men sincerely interested in helping one another learn that no one can help another who is not himself possessed by a divine passion, which feels that in the unseen sphere outside the petty world is to be found the fulcrum on which the leverage of a mighty love can lift the world?

This is the field which is the Church's very own. The church does not constitute society; nor is it meant as a social opportunity. It is not an academy; it is not a club for mere entertainment; its building is not a concert hall; its minister is not a controversialist; it is not organized as a convenient aid to civil security. It is the company whose religion is *a passionate devotion to the will of God*, whose worship is *each one going out of himself to discover what that will appoints*, and to whom "conduct is more than three-fourths of life,"—it is the sphere, undivided and unimpaired, in which life manifests itself.

The Universe is God thinking His thoughts in the terms of matter. It is the body of that never-absent mind. As surely as this is true and gives consistency to the physical order, so surely is it true that a man in spiritual affinity with this eternal Mind will think the thoughts of God, and will form about his vital being not the system of ethics, which, when most complete, is the matching together artificially and mechanically of bits of external life, but he will think the beautiful thoughts of God in the terms of a beautiful life.

This seems to me the point of view from which to regard *the Church as a School of Ethics*. From this point of view ethics take the wider sense of life,—life as deep in its source as the deep of being, as loving in its temper as the heart of God, which is the heart of the world.

RELIGION AND DEMOCRACY

BY REV. HOWARD N. BROWN

OF BROOKLINE, MASSACHUSETTS

ONE of the finest sayings of recent times, and one that may serve as a kind of text for the line of thought to which I invite your attention, is to be found in an address delivered by our late Minister to England, shortly before his departure from that country. "Democracy," said Mr. Lowell, "does not mean, 'I am as good as you are:' it means, 'You are as good as I am.'" Among the lavish expressions of extravagant hope, on the one hand, and of irrational fear, on the other, which the growth of this new power, called "Democracy," provokes, it is good to hear, now and again, a word of sanity and wisdom which sheds actual light upon our situation. Most thoughtful Americans have proceeded far enough with the experiment in self-government to which they are committed, to be aware that the problems and difficulties, once regarded as the peculiar property of "effete monarchies," have not been left so far behind by our free society as ardent Fourth-of-July orators have supposed. But, ready as we are to confess that democracy has its disadvantages, and certain as it is that the sovereign people are no more infallible than individual kings have proven, yet we have not lost our confidence that free institutions will ultimately justify themselves in the eyes of all mankind; and, though we may not be able to answer our critics convincingly, we know that they who look upon the rise of democracy as the sure death of all that is fair and good have no better eye to criticise the "spirit of the age" than they who do nothing but sing hymns of exultation and adoration before that young giant, as to a new-born deity.

One of the most common apprehensions with regard to the advance of democracy is that it will prove unfavorable to the growth of eminent individual character and ability, and will reduce life to one dead level of mediocrity. It is this fear that the saying I have quoted is designed to correct. "How will you develop great men and distinguished women in a society which offers no secure or lasting reward to exceptional merit?" we are asked. "Have you not taken away much of the incentive which inspires to noble deeds, when your hero knows that only for one brief hour can he command the public notice, and must then pass into a gallery of extinct celebrities, where he suffers all the pains of obscurity, with none of its blessings? Add to this that the moment a man succeeds in winning public favor there are multitudes who hold it as a personal grievance against him, as if he had usurped their place or were standing in their light, and is it any marvel if the best minds study how to evade public notice rather than to secure for themselves name and fame?" Truly, if democracy should prove to mean nothing more than "I am as good as you are," if its distinctive traits could be summed up in the opportunity it offers those who have no light in themselves to try the effect of dethroning the stars and of elevating their darkness to the place of divine effulgence, then would liberty appear one of the worst delusions that ever lured men to their ruin.

But here is one watchman upon our walls who gives us a more encouraging report; and we are well assured that what he speaks is no mere flourish of rhetoric, but a sober and intelligent judgment, based upon well-ascertained facts. Democracy, he tells us, is not, primarily, the impudent attempt which ignorance often makes to establish its equality with wisdom, but is, rather, the willing disposition of those who are strong to lift up and dignify the life of the weak. It is no rude fashion, on the part of the multitude, of shouldering the individual out of its path, but the growth of a courteous inclination in every man to yield his neighbor the favored side of the way. Figuring the social scale as a long flight of steps which humanity is engaged in mounting, we may say that the essential aim of free institutions is to stop the attempt made by those who occupy a higher level to bar the advance of those beneath, and induce them, instead, to reach out a friendly hand toward the occupants of lower station. All this, if democracy truly means, "You are as good as I am;" if its ruling spirit is that of mutual helpfulness and respect, not one of unbridled jealousy and loose irreverence. For it is plain that, to secure peace and order upon this great stairway of social ranks and grades, there must be both a willingness to make room on the upper steps for those who are able to climb and a respectful attitude on the part of those beneath for such forms of human worth as have risen higher than they. There will be from above not much invitation to "come up higher," while from below rises the snarling mandate to "step down and give place to others." On either side, the truce may be fatally broken. In presence of a surging mob, which seeks to capture positions of command for the sake of "spoils" and which has no reverence for the responsibilities of office, authority must barricade its doors. On the other hand, if they who dwell upon the summits of society build walls and establish sentinels about their habitation, thus converting into their private castle what should be an open goal for the general ambition, the masses of men will inevitably declare war against them. Though, as the proverb reminds us, "it takes two to make a quarrel," yet, in this present world, one party can usually contrive, without great trouble, to force the quarrel; and we get no assurance of peace till on both sides we have established a peaceable disposition. A society whose meaning can be truly interpreted by the phrase, "You are as good as I am," implies, therefore, not only the abolition of barriers of caste by which humble merit is prevented from rising to honorable estate, but the subordination of that swaggering tendency of inferior human nature, which says, always, "I am as good as you." It means a condition of things in which the stronger elements of life are willing to take the burden of helping on the feebler, and in which superior knowledge and virtue are not balked of their charitable intent through the lawless and suspicious hostility of place-hunting humanity.

It is probably unnecessary to correct a possible misapprehension in the English mind, growing out of Mr. Lowell's speech, by confessing that on this side the water we have not arrived at the full bliss of democratic perfection, as thus interpreted. Democracy, as the finished product of forces now at work, the final outcome of changes now being effected, may prove itself all that a poet's fancy could demand. But democracy, at some half-way point in its making, which is about as far as we may claim to have reached, has numerous other phrases on its lips besides those which indicate the respect of man for man. Free society, as we know it to-day, is a strangely-blended mixture of selfishness and public spirit, of charity and brutality; and, judging solely by the evidence presented, without faith to help us out, we are not always sure which factor has the ascendency. Mingled with the better life, which cares for the honor of the nation and regards free institutions as a sacred trust, there is another element, to which the "American opportunity" is simply that of a glutton at a free banquet,— to gorge himself to the utmost possible extent. Too often, the ruder mind aspires only to the joy and comfort of looking down upon its fellows from a superior elevation, lacks entirely the habit of reverence for mental and moral attainments greater than its own. Too many conceive themselves defrauded of their natural right to rise by spiritual wickedness in high places, and instead of patient attempts to deserve promotion devote their energies to violent assaults upon the chief seats and their occupants. Too often, cultivation, refinement, and wealth cut themselves off from sympathy with all life that is not able to conform to their standards, look upon it as an insolence if, in any particular, the humble ape the manners of the great, and appear to regard poverty either as a necessary foil to their splendor or as the divinely ordained emptiness wherein their golden alms may ring with proper sound. Much as there is, in the life of our people, of respect for law and order and of appreciation for true nobility and worth, there is also enough disbelief in the reality of virtue, enough persuasion that reform is nothing but a cloak to selfishness and greed, enough insolence, irreverence, and impious assumption that heaven stands on terms of equality with the pit, to amaze and disgust at times even the most ardent champion of the rights of man. And, if we turn to higher quarters, one sees that the keen-witted and strong may and do construe the gospel of human brotherhood in widely different ways; for, while in one place the abler kind of humanity beholds the less fortunate as children of its own Father in heaven, and recognizes its brotherly obligation to afford help, another sort says, flatly, "Being our equals before God, take care of yourselves as we do, and do not hang upon us like incapable animals." There are ears to which the pathetic appeal of the common workman, "You employ our hands as if they were tools of wood or steel, and care nothing for our hearts or our souls," sounds only as the whine or snarl of a wicked discontent. There are minds supposing themselves to be gifted with great penetration which fail to note underneath the self-assertion of humbler classes the piteous appeal of those who do not know, to be taught how they shall make more of the life God has given them. We have with us representatives of what Carlyle was wont to call "gigmanity,"—a class whose philosophy of life is built upon the fundamental belief that to all the virtuous Heaven grants a two- or four-wheeled chaise, and that every man who trudges along through the dust is justly condemned to that fate for his sins.

All this, of course, means that we must note in our midst the growth of both a true and a false democracy. Under free institutions, as everywhere else, while there is one mental disposition to be gentle with weakness and respectful toward virtue, we have to do with another bullying sort of human nature, which lets no chance slip to play the tyrant, and never concedes that anybody is better than itself. Civil liberty grants a fair field and no favor to both these types; and it should go without saying that, if, in the end, the latter proves strong enough to stamp our democracy as a whole with its peculiar impress, our sign among the nations will be anything but beautiful or sublime. Let but that part of the mind of the nation which is fitted for leadership grow hopeless or careless of its duties to the Commonwealth; let the baser instincts of men gain courage to turn an entirely deaf ear to those counsels of wisdom and purity which they already declare to be nothing more than the cant of hypocrisy; let the demagogue, whose power is far too threatening as it is, once gather the art of statesmanship into his keeping,—and history has plenty of instructive examples to teach us what will be the end of our attempt at self-government.

Now, we have an amount of faith in our manifest destiny which is a terribly discouraging obstacle in the way of an alarmist. Even in the excitement of a political campaign, nobody more than half believes in the tremendous crisis that is always proclaimed, because we have imbibed with our mother's milk a confiding trust in the republic, which nothing seriously disturbs. But that faith sometimes shows itself too much like the shiftless optimism of Mr. Wilkins Micawber, and depends too exclusively upon things that are expected to "turn up" in the nick of time, to be rated as either very reasonable or very moral by thinking people. If, knowing our weakness, we can see also its remedy, and be sure of our ability to make a practical and efficient application that, surely, were better than any amount of blind reliance upon a supposed fatality of greatness, that may be expected to buoy us up. It is not without strong persuasion of the possibility of such an intelligent faith in the future that I have called attention to the chief obstacle in our way.

The problem is, briefly put, how to keep knowledge and ignorance working together for the common good. The danger is that ignorance, preferring its delusions or suspecting selfish designs in the advice of the better informed portion of the community, and holding its social superiors rather than its own lack of capacity responsible for the pinch in its lot, will grow to listen to nothing but the devices of its own darkened understanding. The belief that this must be the natural outcome of democracy made Carlyle fierce against it; and, for my part, I cannot discover that they who have abused Carlyle for his distrust have done much to show wherein he was wrong. I take it that in every city and village and township there are intelligent and cautious citizens whose words ought to have weight with their neighbors, and, lacking whose influence, the life of these localities would suffer serious decline.

To be sure, it may be said that experience is the great teacher of mankind, and that when people do not know the path, after they have broken their heads against stone walls a sufficient number of times, they will at last blunder into the right and open way. But such trust in a happy issue, where the blind lead the blind, ignores the ditch which divine Providence has especially prepared for those who regard eyesight as a superfluous gift. The hope of the republic is that whatever of mental or moral vision the life of the people may produce will come to the front, and will find its way into the ranks of leadership more surely and speedily than in other forms of society. To base our hope upon the notion that lower grades of intelligence do not need to be instructed, but, in default of all sound teaching from human sources, will be inspired by Heaven to conduct their affairs sagaciously, is to build upon the flimsiest of all foundations. In every place, what is said by the most far-seeing, the best informed and most capable, ought to be listened to with respect, and should have great weight in shaping public opinion. But men who possess these qualities will generally, perhaps, be capitalists or the friends of capitalists. What, then, if, in his mad enmity toward the possessors of wealth and social position, the common laborer, more and more, refuses to be guided by those who are competent to lead, and inclines to a course exactly opposite to the one they recommend? We may grant that the average mind is of right our jury, by whom the verdict is to be made up. But how if the jury resolve to try the case themselves, without the help of judge and counsel? Or suppose they listen to the law and evidence laid down to them, under the fixed impression that the court is doing its best to lead them astray, and that they ought, as far as possible, to decide against it on every point? With that idea in their heads, our jury are like to become a very indifferent oracle of justice.

Such being the nature of our difficulty, we take one clear step of advance upon it, when we discover that it rests, at last, with the stronger intelligence to say what the disposition of weaker minds shall be toward its authority. We may lay it down as an established lesson of history that every revolt of a people against those who are set to be its captains and guides means infidelity to their trusts on the part of these leaders themselves. Ignorance does not rise in rebellion while it has confidence that its teachers are laboring for its good, nor until it has come to realize in bitterness of spirit that these advisers and governors have no interest in its welfare, and only use it for their own advantage. Then ignorance does rebel, and ought to rebel; and all the revolutions and conflagrations it may occasion are justified by the necessity of finding rulers who are not mere leeches upon the body politic, but hold their office to enrich and enlighten the general life. This is why democracy must mean, " You are as good as I am," and can mean nothing else, if it would keep itself alive. Let those who have the ability and the means apply themselves, in patriotic zeal, to work out the problems of social and political life, showing a philanthropy which desires to elevate every human soul; and they shall find the people willing to be taught. Let them, on the other hand, produce the impression that they care for nothing but to push their own fortunes, and are at heart indifferent to the welfare of their fellow-men, and the rude hand of the public will gladly avail itself of

the first opportunity to deal them a staggering blow.
If, as sometimes happens, we are brought into contact
with a kind of humanity which seems unable to appreciate what is being done for it, we should remember
how many immigrants have come to us out of countries
where a landed nobility feel hardly any closer bond between themselves and their peasantry than that which
binds them to their horses or their dogs. After a race
of people has lain for ages under the feet of a respectability shod with iron and brass, it is not to be expected
that the children of this people will walk erect, without
manifesting some suspicion toward whatever wears the
dress of their traditional foe. But, apart from this imported stock of rebellious instinct, which we may hope
our atmosphere will gradually dissipate, I hold it to be
almost an axiom concerning human nature that it will
honor and trust the natural authority of wisdom and
purity wherever that authority reaches out the hand of
a kindly and brotherly intent. They who occupy stations which should give them influence over the minds
and consciences of others have it in their own power to
decide whether they will use or throw away their opportunity. The question of peace or war between them
and the classes which need their help is for them to determine. They have but to adopt a policy of selfishness, denunciation, and disdain, and all prospect of their
being able to exercise the functions of leadership at
once vanishes. But, if they can be induced to adopt as
their motto this phrase, "You are as good as I am;" if
they can be taught that the bonds of our common humanity are more real than class distinctions, and can be
depended upon to carry forward, with unfailing pa-

tience, the great task of public enlightenment,—then, and only then, are we safe from the anarchy and license which must always lie close upon the borders of a free society.

And, now, what principle or power planted within the domain of intellectual life will keep the best thought and intelligence of the nation consecrated to the work which God has given them to do? What will hold the gifts whereby men rise to power over their fellows in the service of humanity, and prevent them from being diverted to the mere selfish interest of their owners?

I answer, It must be the power of sentiment, and that so deeply touched by the consciousness of something sacred and divine in human life that it amounts to a religious sentiment. We have words to indicate what that power is, in essence, upon which democracy, of all forms of society, makes largest demands,—philanthropy, the love of men; patriotism, the filial tie which binds the sons of the soil to their common fatherland. The nation is a larger family; and its prosperity, like the peace of our households, rests upon a basis of deep and pure emotion. There can be no question, as between the perceptions of the head and the feelings of the heart, which is the wider and more commanding power. We build upon the surface of life our structures of the understanding, lay down our swiftly-travelled lines of logic or essay the navigation of the air in our balloon-like theories. But, through and around the whole compass and circumference of these superficial creations, the force, as of gravitation, which binds our human lives together and holds them up in their pathway, is the force of sentiment.

We recognize this perfectly in our homes. The love which establishes order and harmony in the domestic circle is no product of a shrewd calculation as to the results of self-sacrifice, and does not derive its strength from intellectual beliefs or definitions. It is a voice of nature which comes from a source deeper than the reasoning faculties, and which often sets them at defiance. We educate our children, and seek the happiness of our brethren and kindred, not alone nor principally because we think it will pay, but because affection delights in the health and joy of those it holds dear. So, in the wider relations of society and the State, duty still needs to be strongly rooted in the soil of sentiment, to give it life and power. The attachment of men to that form of government under which they have been reared, what we call the loyalty of a people, is much more than the selfish interest of each one to maintain the means of livelihood, and would be a very poor resource in time of public danger, if it could be estimated in dollars and cents. There are heats of patriotic feeling under which the universal heart quivers with the intensity of its hopes and fears, as under no expectation of loss or gain in personal estate. There is a capacity in human nature to give its hoarded treasure as freely as if it had no value, and to pour out its blood like water in defence of the nation's liberties. It is by virtue of its ability to command such sacrifices from its citizens that a government is strong; nor can it boast much stability, unless the hearts of men do so cling to it as to the mother that bore them. This respect of man for man, of which we have been speaking,—what is it, in its last analysis, but a feeling? And how shall it be cultivated otherwise than as a feeling, by appeals that stimulate the emotional part of our nature? In other words, if we are to pay to our neighbor any real tribute of honor and deference, it must be a kind of religion with us to yield him our respect. On compulsion of an inward desire so to express ourselves, and irrespective of the reasons to be assigned, we must love men, as we pray to God, because that is the natural and inevitable utterance of our being, or duties of charity of hospitality and brotherhood have no great hold upon us. It is one thing to trace out the explanation of those courses which the higher life of mankind adopts: it is quite another thing to have that life flowing abundantly through the pulsations of one's own soul. We may see never so clearly the line of action that we should follow; but have we the will and courage and desire to support us in that pathway? At bottom, it is always a question of the amount and quality of life that we possess to sustain our impulses of love and hope and ambition. And, therefore, it is a question of religion. For religion is life, or, at lowest, the imitation of what was once alive. It is that utterance of himself to which man is impelled, in view of the sublime and mysterious qualities of existence that force themselves upon his consciousness.

Like religion, and of its substance and flavor,—both as springing from depths of life below the understanding, and as recognizing an Infinite and Eternal Power at work in the life of humanity,—must be Democracy's confession of faith, "You are as good as I am," if that phrase is to represent a force of control commensurate with our need. That immense and somewhat irrational confidence in the republic, of which I have before spoken, is, perhaps, a rudimentary religion in the soul of our young democracy. Certainly, we may so name it, if, beyond the fact that we are big and free, it contains a dawning sense of divine and glorious promises to be fulfilled through our success, and of an everlasting wisdom which works with us to secure a happy issue from our struggles and conflicts. But, unless we feel so strongly the divine meaning and purpose of our gospel of civil and religious liberty that we are perforce made its apostles and defenders, we have not attained the religion of democracy. That is only a half faith which says, "This is the Lord's work, let Him attend to it." When the soul has a real perception of the coming kingdom of heaven, it cries, "This is God's truth; and woe is me if I preach it not from the housetop!"

The only power competent to keep our best intellects devoted to the service of humanity, and out of Napoleonic schemes for selfish dominion, is of this character. The strong bearing the burdens of the weak as a kind of wholesome moral exercise is not a particularly hopeful or exhilarating spectacle. Duties which are to be classed as belonging to that surface world of fashion, custom, or expediency, are not in themselves currents of vital energy, but are more like those bars and shoals of sand which a great river produces and shifts about in its bed, with continual effort to sweep them out of its way. Methods or morals, to be significant of great things, must be rooted and grounded in the life itself. Like the growth of a tree, they must be the outward expression of an inward principle of force, which exists only to do its own appropriate work, and which the whole universe cannot persuade to bear other than its own fruit. This it is which makes a man's religion. This is what binds the soul, as the planets are bound in their orbits; and by such might must democracy be drawn and compelled toward its ideal, if it is to prove the stable and beneficent order of mankind's advance through coming ages.

One more point I desire to urge briefly upon your notice, which is that some vital relation exists, or ought to be maintained, between the religious disposition of men, touching their civil and political obligations, and that religion which has its home in our churches. At first glance, it may seem wildly improbable that a religion which appeals very largely to the selfish side of human nature, and calls so loudly upon each individual to escape from the doom of misery to which it has consigned the vast majority, should have much power to kindle sentiments of devotion to the good of humanity. But Christianity has always a better spirit in its heart than finds expression through its doctrines. The example and teaching of its founder make constant protest in the souls of men against the heathenish inheritance of rites and charms designed for private safety, which has been foisted upon the Church. We have reason to be devoutly grateful that our churches are better than their theology, and that, while they are endeavoring to plant in each mind the fruitless question, "How is it with my soul?" they stir the soil for a nobler growth of unselfish interest in the lives of others. Though formal religion does not as yet directly address itself with any great weight of emphasis to the stimulation of that love of man for man which was, perhaps, the chief motive force of early Christianity, yet, in so far as it kindles any life of spiritual ambition and desire, it quickens the sources of that impulse in obedience to which a man will "lay down his life" for his friend, and helps to strengthen the point at which democracy is weak. Strike one note of a harp, and you get a response from all other strings that are in harmony with it. Touch anywhere the deep chords of spiritual feeling in man's heart, and the vibration runs through them all. Such religion as we have is by no means an idle display of useless sentiment, and we may depend upon it to be of great service to us in keeping alive the fires of patriotism and of enthusiasm for humanity's advance.

But imagine a church which has cast aside the hopeless theories that have rendered the outlook of so many Christians more dismal and pessimistic than that of any so-called pagan faith, to draw its inspiration from belief that the divine image can be revealed in every soul, and that human nature everywhere is designed and destined to be filled with the spirit of God! Imagine a church in which the saints no longer look down in scorn and wrath upon the sinners, but where the most spotless Pharisee is taught to recognize and value what is good in the meanest publican; a church which says to all mankind, "I make no pretence of being your master, and ask only to be your servant,"—should not that church greatly help democracy to its true profession,— "You are as good as I am,"—and bring to bear upon the national life most powerful incentives to mutual helpfulness and respect? I think the world waits and longs for such a worship of God as beholds His presence in every form that His life has quickened, and loves to lift up from the dust the humanity which, in its lowest degradation, bears some trace of the graces and beauties of heaven. When, in our churches, a religion of this kind is preached and cultivated, then there will be, over all the great field of life, guidance for the blind and help for the overladen; and liberty shall then imply the swift and orderly march of mankind's vast army to those high places whither it has long been beckoned.

THE SIMPLICITY OF THE GOSPEL

BY REV. ANDREW P. PEABODY, D.D.

OF CAMBRIDGE, MASSACHUSETTS

AFTER more than half a century's conversance with the various and successive forms of scepticism as to the authenticity of the Gospels, I feel a stronger faith than even that of my unquestioning childhood in these books as a substantially truthful record of the life and mission of Jesus Christ. At the same time I am more than ever profoundly impressed with the simplicity of his method, teachings, and spirit, and with the injury that has been done to Christianity and the vantage-ground that has been given to sceptics and infidels by the foisting upon it of technical theology. No word has been so much abused or has done so much mischief as *doctrine*. It is not, properly speaking, a Christian word. It is used, indeed, in our translation of the New Testament, but always as equivalent to a Greek word which means not dogma, but moral teaching. Thus St. Paul tells servants to adorn the doctrine, that is, the teaching of God their Saviour by not stealing from their masters; and I might quote a half-score or more of passages from which it would appear that what we call duties are the doctrines of the New Testament, so that we use only its own language when we term the Sermon on the Mount a summary of Christian doctrine. Indeed, Christianity has no doctrines in our sense of the word,—no technical or formal statements as to the subjects on which Christians have been disputing for these many centuries. The subjects of these disputes form no part of Christ's teaching, nor yet, as it seems to me, of that of either of the sacred writers. St. Paul is commonly quoted for them, and he does employ a good many words and phrases that seem technical; but he uses them only in controversy with Judaizing Christians, and it was necessary for him to use words designating their beliefs and the relation of his own to them. Thus, were I to hold a controversy with a Swedenborgian, I should, of necessity, employ a large amount of the peculiar phraseology of the New Church in designating the points of resemblance and difference between its beliefs and mine. It is only in controversy that St. Paul uses these terms, and they have, therefore, come into the Christian Church, though through a Christian medium, not from a Christian source, but from the dialect of the synagogue and the rabbis.

We may reach our best conception of Christ's actual mission and work by supposing the appearance of a similar personage in our own time and land,—of not merely a very good man, but of one who gave manifest tokens of pre-eminent endowments as a teacher, a reformer, a builder, a restorer of our moral waste and desolation, the author of a new reign of honesty, purity, benevolence, and piety. What should we expect of him? Not surely a creed or a ritual, but rather a stout iconoclasm of existing creeds and rituals so far as they are made tests of character, grounds of separation, or substitutes for active duty and vital godliness. He would go to our seat of government, and denounce, in terms of intensest indignation, time-serving, faithlessness, and peculation. He would go among those whose sole aim is selfish gain, and would expose the morbid anatomy of the heart that has for its only treasure that which can be lost or stolen, and which must be left behind in dying. He would go among the sensual and debauched, and demonstrate the living death, the gangrene, the gnawing of the earth-worm, of which they are perishing. He would go among the formalistic teachers of religion who leave fashionable sin and respectable evil unrebuked, and would lay bare the latent hypocrisy that lurks wherever men's meanness and guilt are condoned for their conformity to church creeds or ecclesiastical observances. He would ferret out wrong and sin in their subterfuges and disguises, and drag them forth into the clear light of the divine presence and judgment. Nor would he content himself with the superficial treatment of moral evil or with its surface-reform. He would track it out in all its windings to its source in the unconsecrated will, in the autonomy of a selfish aim, in slavery to the senses and the outward life, and the neglect and oblivion of the God-born, spiritual, immortal nature.

In this work he would bring to bear upon men's souls not formal dogmas, but truths simple as vast, truths as old as the creation, truths which a child could understand, but which the wisest men could not exhaust or transcend,—the venerable presence and unslumbering love of God, His omnipresent and inevitable law, the righteous retribution that awaits in full all the good and all the evil of men's hearts and lives, the reaching out of that retribution into the unseen and eternal future, the certainty that sin can have no place of privilege anywhere or anywhen in God's universe, but must ever bear its growing burden of shame and misery.

In urging these truths on men's hearts and consciences he would use not a vocabulary of his own, but the language which he found current, the epithets which meant the most in the ears of his hearers, the metaphors and comparisons which would flash conviction on them the most vividly, the modes of appeal which would most assuredly startle them into penitence and wake into life the dormant germs of a nobler selfhood. Let his words be written down, there would be many of his utterances which would not bear to be interpreted by the grammar and the dictionary, or in the way in which lawyers interpret the words of a statute,—many of them which, thus interpreted, would seem inconsistent with one another, and might give rise to endless disputes and conflicting parties, yet which, interpreted by the time, place, occasion, and surroundings, would all harmonize, and would appear to be different ways of adapting the same truths to different types and measures of receptivity.

It is thus that we are to regard the mission of Jesus as a teacher and a reformer. His was, indeed, a worldwide and a world-enduring work; but it was first to be wrought upon the men of his own time and nation, and through them to be diffused and transmitted among all nations and to the end of time. He used the language of his age and people,—an oriental dialect, abounding in bolder personifications and metaphors than are common in the western tongues,—a hybrid of the Hebrew and Chaldee, which had a scanty vocabulary,—often compared by contrast, affirmed by negation, and for lack of more fitting terms employed strong material imagery to convey spiritual ideas. He had hearers who, for many generations, had lapsed into an hereditary dulness of apprehension, had become dead to the sublime significance of psalm and prophecy, and could be aroused only by vivid word-pictures almost visible to the outward eye, by startling appeals, by realistic representations intensified to the utmost capacity of language. Now such teachings, literally interpreted, especially with obscure passages of the Pauline writings employed as a commentary, might easily give birth to dogmas both entirely alien to their actual import and spirit, and mutually incompatible and destructive.

Let us take a single instance of this kind. One who receives Christ's teachings as to the immeasurable love and universal fatherhood of God cannot rest in the belief that an infinitely good being can doom any of his children to unending torment, and yet from the literal interpretation of some of Christ's words that doom has been assigned not only to all nominal Christians who fall short of the arbitrary standard of a particular sect, but to the myriads that have never had the opportunity of knowing the Gospel, to non-baptized persons whether adults or infants (including the long array of Quaker saints who have been the pre-eminently close followers of Christ), nay, even to all who have died in infancy and early childhood, to whom the Puritan divine and poet, Michael Wigglesworth, makes the Judge assign "the easiest room in hell,"—thus investing the God and Father of the Lord Jesus Christ with attributes which would well fit our conception of Moloch, of Juggernaut, or of Satan.

Now the whole spirit of Christ's teaching is opposed to such a belief. The child whom Jesus held up to his disciples as a symbol of the regenerate soul had certainly not been baptized, and yet such as he have, by high ritualists, been denied Christian burial and a resting-place in consecrated ground. The shepherd in the parable gives himself no rest till he has brought back the one wandering sheep to his fold. The father goes out to meet the prodigal son, instead of awaiting his return.

But Jesus aptly uses the very strongest terms that oriental imagery can furnish to rouse the obdurate and impenitent from their guilty and perilous security. They are rushing to destruction. They are committing spiritual suicide. Their guilt is a consuming fire, which can never be quenched so long as they furnish it fuel, whether in this world or in the world to come. Could he have said less? What moral teacher has not used similar language, as intense and vivid, if allowance be made for the difference of idiom? I have often said to a young man, "You are going to certain ruin as fast as you can go; you are destroying yourself, body and soul." But I never added, "If you go on in this way a few years longer, and then take a different course, all will be well with you," nor, "If you go on in this way as long as you live on earth, the discipline of another state of being may set you right." This, through the mercy of God, may be true; but it is no part of the truth needed "for reproof, for correction, for instruction in righteousness." What the sinner needs is that he be made to feel that so long as he remains as he is there is no future for him save the blackness of darkness ever deepening, whether on the hither or on the farther side of the grave. This is precisely Christ's method with sinners. His purpose is to call them to immediate repentance, not to invite them to a vague trust in the possibilities of an unknown future, in the purging fires of a probation in another world. He makes it as certain as words can make it that for the sinner to cease to be a sinner is the essential condition of the divine favor and of heavenly happiness. We cannot imagine a teacher from God, or a man of virtuous sense and feeling, or any but a thoroughly immoral person, as laying out through hell a highway to heaven, or as treating sin otherwise than as imminent destruction, repentance otherwise than as an urgent necessity.

If we examine Christ's method throughout, we shall see that it is never by technical dogmas, but by the presentation of fundamental truths as God's message through him, that he seeks to renovate, save, and bless humanity; and they are truths, any one of which, brought home to our souls, as they were thrown by him in living light-beams on men's consciences, would make us all that we ought to be. Thus could we feel as we believe the divine presence, could we go about with the sense of that ever-open eye upon our inmost souls, would there not be a constraining, shaping, hallowing influence on our whole inward being, from which our lips would ever speak, and our lives flow, in the beauty of holiness? Or could we take in the revelation of the Father's love, as, even more than in the order and beauty of nature, it outrays itself in him who was that love incarnate, could we fail to render in faithful duty our constant tribute of thanksgiving and praise? Or could we feel the reality of that measured and inevitable retribution on which Jesus so constantly dwells, could we dare to forsake the only life-way on which there rests the faintest ray of hope? Above all, could we feel the blessedness and loveliness of the great Teacher's life and spirit, the intensity of his compassion, the gentleness, tenderness, sweetness of his walk among men, the power of his cross, the majesty and mercy of those hours of agony, could we withhold from him the fruit of his soul-travail, or refrain from making ourselves a living sacrifice to him who made himself "the sacrifice of our peace"? These are the spiritual forces through which Jesus moves the world, through which his redeeming, transforming ministry has come down through the ages, and in which he stands at the door of our hearts and demands admission there.

These forces are belittled and shorn of their strength when cramped into what are commonly called doctrines. Moreover, it is the doctrine-forming and the doctrine-believing tendency, rather than the character of the doctrines, that does harm. We talk of false doctrines, erroneously it may be; for in many cases it is not the falsity of the doctrine so much as its being a doctrine, that is to be deprecated. We profess to reject such and such doctrines, almost always to our loss and injury. Their falsity generally consists in their being partial and inadequate definitions of the truth which they profess to represent, and we are prone, in our zeal for the truth, to ignore or deny not only the doctrines which are false merely in form, but their underlying concepts, which are profoundly true. While I regard the portion of the Christian Church with which I am associated as my religious home, in which, as I was born and baptized in it, I hope to stay so long as I have a home on earth, I am more and more impressed with the belief that all the leading sects of Christians have a just claim on our regard for the very dogmas in which they seem most to differ from us; for there is hardly one of those dogmas which is not the maimed or distorted reflection of some truth which we neglect or ignore only to our cost and detriment.

Indeed, opposite dogmas, whose partisans used to burn each other, and are as near doing so now as the age will let them, are almost always, while equally false as dogmas, equally true in the principles which they respectively represent, limit, and mutilate, but which are as opposite poles of a magnet with a connecting wire. Thus, in the old time, Augustine and Pelagius started the conflict which has not yet ceased between human freedom and man's moral inability, both false as exclusive and limiting dogmas, both true in the synthesis in which St. Paul unites them when he says, "Work out your own salvation with fear and trembling; for it is God that worketh in you to will and to do of His good pleasure."

I sympathize with my whole heart with the purpose and spirit of the Protestant Reformation, and the dogmas which the reformers repudiated were and are, as dogmas, false and revolting, belittling and sometimes debasing to God and man. But there underlie these very dogmas truths which Protestantism is impoverished by ignoring, and which give to the piety of enlightened and devout Romanists a heavenly glow and charm, rendering much of their religious literature and biography transcendently edifying. Let me explain what I mean, and in so doing I shall best illustrate the distinction between dogmas and their underlying truths. Jesus expressed, as it seems to me, not only what his disciples should behold, but what he meant should be the experience of all his followers, when he said, "Henceforth ye shall see heaven open, and the angels of God ascending and descending upon the Son of man." He lived under the opened heavens, in incessant communion with the unseen world, and he meant that his disciples should thus live. His great aim was to rend the veil away,—to make of the two worlds one world, of the family in heaven and on earth one family. The early Christians, in their times of purity, persecution, and martyrdom, maintained this heavenly converse, this transcendental consciousness. They felt themselves citizens of the heavenly city, while dwelling as strangers and pilgrims in this world. Their writings, their utterances on the cross and at the stake, their entire life-record, attest the reality of this double, interbraided consciousness. But when Christianity mounted the throne of the Cæsars, and bishops became courtiers, and the Church a temporal sovereignty, these heavenly experiences died out of men's hearts, without being expunged from their creeds. They became sacred traditions, embodied in rituals, cramped and frozen into dogmas,—truths so narrowed and travestied as to be falsities. Hence the institution of formal prayers to the Madonna and to saints and angels, the pretence of specifically efficacious intercession for souls in purgatory, the doctrine of indulgences from the treasury of supererogatory merit earned by the saints, in fine, the entire system by which the Church became a mercenary bureaucracy for transactions between earth and heaven, —a system so glaringly absurd, so grossly mischievous, that the alternative of purifying it and restoring it to its primitive simplicity seems hardly to have presented itself to Calvin and his associates, and to others like Luther appeared only a desirable impossibility. The consequence was in all Protestantism, and for the most part down to the present time, the rehanging of the veil between the two worlds, the relegation of the Holy Spirit to the day of Pentecost or to special seasons of outpouring at uncertain intervals, the postponement of heaven till after death, the non-recognition of fellowship between those living on earth and those more truly living in the inner courts of the Father's house, and in the faith of not a few the virtual suspension of retribution for good and evil till some far-off day of judgment. The gain was indeed great as regards the fetichism of saint and image worship and the mercantile relations with heaven, that were superseded. But the loss was equally great as to the consciousness of heavenly communion from which these superstitions sprang. The more spiritual of the Romanists, while still observing the forms of their church, to them types of better things, evidently revert in consciousness to the condition of the earlier church, own the presence of the cloud of unseen witnesses, consciously blend their praises and their prayers with the worship of the heavenly host, and regard heaven and earth as but different apartments of the same house of God, in which from room to room are doors and avenues along which may pass mutual sympathies, intercessions, and thanksgivings.

It is to be most profoundly regretted that the Romeward movement in the English Church should not have been arrested at this point. But there again we see the old tendency to pervert communion into formalism, aspiration into dogma, and to replace glowing faith in things unseen by hard and fast affirmations about things seen. Thus a new sect has been virtually created in the bosom of the Anglican Church.

This is but one illustration of the sect-making that is perpetually going on. The process may be described somewhat as follows: A great truth is reflected from some mirror of human consciousness. The mirror is of limited extent, and dim in parts; it is uneven, and its reflecting power is not always the same. The reflection is, therefore, fragmentary, inaccurate, inadequate. If it were taken for what it is, it would be prolonged, renewed, repeated, and pains would be taken to purify, smooth, and polish the mirror. Thus more and more of the truth would be seen. It would present itself under different aspects, in its relations with other truths, at its meeting-points with truths that at first seem its opposites or negatives. Increasing knowledge would thus be acquired, and the feeling would still be, and would urge the believer on to fuller, clearer views, "Lo, these are a part of his ways; but how little a portion is known of him!" But the first reflection is assumed as representing the whole truth, and as excluding all that cannot at once be interpreted as in harmony with it. Thus a dogma is formed, a sect is aggregated about it, and war is waged for and against single portions or aspects of truths which, in a larger view, are mutually consistent, mutually complementary, and will ultimately be the faith of the whole Church, should the time ever come when the Saviour's seamless robe is wrapped over his entire living body.

Meanwhile, it may be that dogma and sect are a need of human infirmity, though of a weakness which we should endeavor to outgrow, and which the Church is now more rapidly outgrowing than thirty years ago the most sanguine optimist would have dared to hope. Pure oxygen is too bracing for the lungs of earth-dwellers, and needs, that it may be safely breathed, to be diluted with more than its weight and bulk of a neutral gas. In like manner, it may be that evangelic truth needs dilution for the imperfect receptivity of many of its most sincere and earnest disciples. We may regard every dogmatic system as corresponding to some peculiar state of mind, to some spiritual diathesis with its special cravings, which must be met by a divine religion, and which only a divine religion can satisfy. He who believes himself under condemnation for Adam's sin must have that stain washed away no less than the soil of his own guilt. He who cannot hope for forgiveness without a literal and full expiation, must find that expiation, else he has no Saviour. He who is incapable of recognizing spiritual worth outside of his own church, must find in a religion that shall meet his wants the precise mode of redemption which that church regards as the only mode, — it may be, in many respects, entirely different from the only mode in which his neighbor imagines that salvation can be, and thinks that it has been, wrought for himself.

Yet in Christianity they all find what they crave, the complement of their conscious imperfections, the deliverance from what they think that they need to be delivered from, the precise key to heaven, with its curiously complicated wards, to which alone, as they suppose, the golden gate will turn. They are all right,—not because the Gospel is vague, but because its truth is vast and all-embracing,—broad enough to comprise every possible need of an earnest and travailing soul, elastic enough to shape itself to every condition of honest belief and profound feeling. It is many-colored, not in its own pure, white radiance, but as refracted through the unnumbered mediums, more or less opaque and of infinitely varied hues, held up between it and the human soul. Were it dogma, it could suit but one grade of minds, satisfy but one class of needs. But because it is life, it can infuse itself wherever there is a craving for life. Because it is omnipotent, it can energize spirits of every type and tone and temper. Because it is Infinite Love, it can lift every burden, solve every doubt, allay every fear, and wrap in its embrace every heaven-seeking soul.

I have spoken of the simplicity of our religion. But let us not confound, as many do, simplicity with shallowness. The principles of Christianity are simple in the same sense in which, and for the same reason for which, the laws of the material universe are simple, because they are fundamental, universal, absolute. They comprehend the entire realm of spirit, all time, all eternity. They have force upon us independently of our choice. By them our destiny is shaping itself now and ever. Now and ever is set the judgment which they reveal.

The books are always open, the book of God's eternal memory and of our own, and we are all the while receiving judgment and sentence for the things that are written in the books, with our places at the right or the left hand of the Judge as truly now as we shall find them when we wake from the death-slumber.

VISIONS AND PATTERNS

BY REV. ROBERT COLLYER

OF NEW YORK

" Look thou, make all things after the pattern which was shown in the mount."—EXODUS xxv. 40.

WE may fairly presume that the Seer did not see the patterns with his eyes or hear what he reports to us with his ears while he sojourned in the Mount of God, but as Milton saw and heard rather, and George Fox and John Bunyan. Milton broods over his "Paradise Lost" until he sees the outlines of the pictures he has painted for us stealing out one by one and falling into their true order. Bunyan follows his Pilgrim on the way to the City of the Saints before he begins to tell the story, or he would have had no heart to begin, and Fox is aware of a shining light where no light shines as yet for other men, and hears voices they cannot hear. And so we must interpret the parable of the vision and the patterns and conclude that these would lie in a few grand and true outlines, overlaid and almost lost in the later ages by what the Master calls the traditions of the elders, and would differ from the work of the seers I have named in this, that while they turned theirs into the things of the Spirit, he would turn these that came to him into things of the purest practical worth to begin with, and then leave them to blossom out in the full time, and bear fruit in the higher life of the nation and the world.

So, if I can understand the story as it touches my text, this was the burden laid on his heart and life. He must come down from his brooding and listening up there, to solve these deep and pregnant problems. How shall I weld those rude families and tribes together into one strong nation? When they have made their way through the wilderness, and settled down and begin to build homes and cities, how shall they make these the abodes of health, and not the breeding-places of plague and pestilence? How shall they find their way to worship as well as work, so that the home, and town, and Church shall be not three but one? These, as I take it, were the problems he must try to solve by God's help and blessing, and as he pondered over them painfully the vision and pattern came to him of such a nation as he would carve out of the rude, rough block which was waiting for him down there on the sands. Of cities so noble by reason of the nobility of the citizen, that they should all be beautiful for situation and the joy of the whole earth. Of a Church which should answer to the need of every man, and woman, and child, and a manhood trained so carefully that for the sake of the whole commonwealth, no man should dare to say, I am my own master and can eat what I will, and drink what I will, and do what I will with my own; I will make my home a sink of foulness or a palace of purity, as I please; wear vile raiment of any sort, or clean and pure robes; go clean, myself, or unclean, as the humor or habit takes me; leave garbage to fester in my door-yard or my drains, or clear it away, and so make things sweet and clean all round. The man I want to find cannot do as he will, the seer says, except as his will stands true to the laws of our human life, for so runs the vision and the pattern. The man must be true and so make the home true, in the city and on the farm, and the home and man true will make the Church true, and the commonwealth. It was a chain he would make like that I saw one day at the jeweller's of twisted links, wrought into a solid strength, four-square, but flexible almost as silk. This was his errand then, as I see him through the mists of time, when he came down from the Mount with the ideals or the outlines of them in his heart,—make the man true by God's blessing, and the home, the Church, and the commonwealth, each bound up with the other, and all needed by each one.

Nor is it hard to see again how he must have the vision and patterns before he began to do the work, dim, it may be, but still growing clear to his inward eye, or there would be no light on his face like that we hear of, and no power in his heart and mind equal to the demand. It would have been then as if Angelo had said before he began to build St. Peter's, I will put in the foundations and then feel my way upward line by line, and finish the thing with a dome or spire, as may seem best. The fine perfection lay in the ideal, in the vision, and patterns. There was the Church as it stole on him out of the dimness; then there was the pattern wrought out line by line, as it must stand forth to the world, in the marble, and then there was St. Peter's, the peerless flower of Christendom.

There had been no such flower if it had not bloomed first in the man's own heart and brain; but when that was once done, the days were too short to answer to his eager desire; nor could the whole ugly might of the Romish ring, just as bad as any we have now, break him down or turn him from his purpose. There it was, the vision and pattern *he* had seen in the mount, and here it must be standing in the sun, and so it must be with this good man and the work God has given him to do. They turn on him and curse him, take their own way, and make common cause with the things that curse them, and are headstrong exactly because they had no head worth the name. But there he stands, as I think of him, looking at the pattern he has seen in the mount, insisting that this is God's word he is saying and God's work he is doing, as these greatest always do, and so it was that through the trouble and frustration which dogged every step of his way from Horeb to Pisgah, he did so manage to mould and inspire those he held in his heart, that in all the world there has been no such race beside. These Jews alone have held their own as a distinct people through all these millenniums of time, and kept abreast of the best life on the earth.

The old supple race they left on the Nile is lost with the broad and burly manhood which built Nineveh and Babylon. The Macedonian who went leaping like fire through the valleys and over the hills that stand about the Jordan, has vanished with the Roman who came after him and drew a furrow over Zion with his ploughshare for a sign. The Saracen has lost his grip who gave them welcome, and the Spaniard who burnt and harried them comes crawling to their feet now and then to beg for a loan to carry on his Government. Nor could I fail to remember when I saw that splendid statue of Lord Beaconsfield in the palace yard at Westminster, how their struggle for existence through more than a thousand years in England had culminated in our time in their giving my mother-land the first real king she has had since Cromwell. A Hebrew man who could whistle the choicest blue blood in the land to his feet wielded the real sceptre and wore the real crown, sent the armies to India and Africa at his will, and bids fair to institute a holy-day, the morrow of St. Primrose.

For good, then, or evil, but for good to my own mind in a vast preponderance, this is the outcome of the vision and patterns. Egypt has sent down her treasure to us, and Greece, and Rome, but the manhood out of which it all came is lost, while the Jew remains. We sing his psalms and pore over his chronicles, and make pilgrimage now to the Holy Land with a devouter heart than his own. His prophecies still stand among the grandest things that ever fell from human lips, and our Gospels, the perfect and peerless flower of all the ages, come to us through his heart.

And so of this wonder I have tried to touch of the vision and patterns was a singular and separate experience, apart and away from your life and mine. I think it would still be well worth our while to take the truth to our hearts; it tells us that we may the better understand how some very wonderful things have been done. But I think it will not be hard to show again how this is not a singular and separate experience; but may be, or, shall I say, must be yours and mine, if we would be well worth our bread and salt in what we have also to do. For, if I may still linger for a moment among the greater lights for help to our smaller, it is to notice that there is always a vision and pattern toward which they strive, who touch us most truly now and sway us most completely, as there was in Milton and Bunyan. "These books of yours are living things," a friend said to the delicate little woman who lived across our moor, in Yorkshire, forty years ago, "how were they done?" "Well," she said, "I brood over them until they *do* live, weeks and months the ideals stay with me, until I feel their living presence, then I wait for the words to become quick with life also as I write them, and so I get my book."

And these are the leafy lanes, I said, the other summer, through which Master Marner went with the linen he had woven for the farmers' wives, and this really may have been his cottage, this place with the pretty garden, and he might have been to me what he was once to the rustics, a rather silly old person of very small account. But she saw him who had a vision as the centre of that sweet blending of our human affections, and the vision of the lost gold came, and then the tangle of golden hair in the firelight, the second treasure that made the first mere dross. It all came to her, she tells us with a certain completeness, it was her ideal, the vision and pattern she saw in the mount, the monograph of loving kindness and tender mercy mastering the selfishness and sin. So it is with all these things that touch us with wonder and delight, and grow finer and better in the ripeness of the years;

there is but one story to tell about the noblest of them and the best, they are born of the vision and answer to the pattern seen in the mount.

Yet if this were the whole truth we might well feel that the most of us could never hope to have part or lot in this great boon, because, so far as we have traced the truth, we have had still to see how only the great ones have the vision who win our hearts by their genius and grace, while we might easily conclude there is nothing left for us to do but to grope along a step at a time, bare of this high grace, and do the best we can with our forlorn chances. This would be a fair objection if it were true, but the truth is our souls also are open to the vision and the pattern as surely as the great ones are I have touched for my instance, and only in this way can we find our choicest direction and inspiration in whatever we have to do which does not end where it begins with the bread that perishes.

I know for myself that thirty-six years ago, when my own life had grown as sad as a November day by reason of the poor chances all about me to make such a home and live such a life as I hungered for in the mother-land, how I brooded over it month after month and then slowly as the day dawns out of the darkness the vision came and the patterns. I saw I must tear out the roots of my young life and plant them again, please God, in the soil of this New World. Then touches of form and color came out of the dimness, not as it is now, but as it might be then, if I made the great adventure. I would tear out the roots of my young life and plant them again, please God, in this New World. I would have a cottage somewhere among the green lanes that skirt your city (for I was country bred), all the children God might give us, sturdy persistence in what I had been trained to do week-days, and a chance to speak of what lay deep and warm in my heart on Sundays. Books for a shilling I must pay a pound for in England, and, alas! I had no pound. Education for the children on ample and easy terms, and finally a vote in the government of the country.

That was my vision and pattern. My old mother wept and said, "My lad, I cannot spare thee. I am a widow and thou art my eldest in thy father's place." "Let me go, mother!" I said, "and you shall not envy the Queen her son."

Good friends, who could not imagine how I could go beyond the drum-tap of England, "Go here," they said, "or there, and we will give you letters and push you on." I knew no man in this New World and had no letters. I did not care,—I was sure if I got here that would be what the pattern called for, and it all came true. The cottage in the green lane and the bit of garden, all the books I wanted, no work to seek in those days, but the work seeking you. The children running about the home; some of them are angels now, and I am trying to think He could not be content, the dear God, to give us only children, but would permit these to come, the blessed ones. Yet I moan "for the touch of a vanished hand" these days, "And the sound of a voice that is still." Home I was saying, schools, work, books, children, they all came right, and they all came true. And now, I say, some such vision and pattern may be caught by any man who will watch for it, and the humbler it may be the better, so that we may be *stormed* now and then by the bounty of heaven, as I have been these many years, above all that we can ask, or think, and say it is not of ourselves, it is the gift of God, not of works, lest any man should boast. And this is my claim that we all stand with this man Moses in these high moments. The vision and pattern never is, or can be, quite the same, but it comes to us all in a mist first, and then if we are true to the inward light and leading we make all things according to that we have seen in the mount. It is the story of the whole world of men and women who have found the truest worth in life, and the truth about which I would allow no doubt or fear. If we will watch and wait, keep the heart humble and trust in God, we all get the patterns. He leaves no man in this great and primal matter to grope in the dark.

And if this is true of the common life it must be true of the higher, which rises out of this as the flower from the root. There is a time for us all, I know, when we can only feel round for what we call the right string. A time of doubt when nothing can be done to a sure and high purpose any more than when this man Moses kept sheep in Midian. But the day comes when the vision comes as the dawn comes, growing a little clearer and giving us the patterns. So it has been with the greatest and the least who have been worth their bread and salt in God's kingdom. God's sovereignty, they call what they have seen, justification by faith, the inward light, the divine fatherhood. It is no matter the truth they stand for grew on them in this old true fashion who are the leaders, and then they went to work to make their ideal actual, and their outlook is ours. It is not the same truth to us all, we are not great enough for that as yet and never may be. And this glass of our own nature may be distorted so that it shall be like those I notice on our street-cars that set all the spires on all the churches toppling over as I ride up the avenue, and I wonder whether those whose mission it seems to be to cry down men like this man of God do not look through some such inward glass at all the church spires. All the same I have yet to meet the man whose mind and heart I could quite respect who could not tell me of a vision and pattern of what religion ought to be, and a religious life. At the very poorest rate, it is a yard measure and a pound weight, and apples as good in the middle of the barrel as at the ends. It is standing by your word and your friend, or between a brute and a little child, or a woman or a horse or a dog. It is being right and doing right, and mercy and pity and charity, and then from these it is the soul that soars and sings right into heaven. I have known a sight of men, the rough men in the shops, and men whose names touch me like a benediction, and I have yet to find the first man who could tell me he has never had his vision and pattern. It comes to the lad through all his wilfulness. It touches the youth with reverence for the noble ideals he sees in others, it comes to us all who can be held responsible for any truth and beauty in our life. Poems, pictures, wonders of worth in every kind, religious and social revolutions, and the making of great saints, all turn on this which he saw with the inward eye in the days of his uplifting. But I say again, these great ones have no patent right to the vision; it is like the sun, which can glass its light in the Atlantic or in the dew-drop trembling in the heart of a violet. How shall I do the work of Him that sent me? How shall I find the one woman in all the world for my wife? Where shall I go if the land is too strait, directed as he was, the father of the faithful, and as surely and as well? How shall we order our home so that it shall be what this man intended the homes of Israel should be, as squared stones and pillars of the Church and the commonwealth? and how shall all these blossom forth bravely into the higher and diviner life? Ask the man who works for you by the day to let you have a look at his patterns, as I was asking old John who tends our furnace, and I tell you, you will wonder, not over his dogmas, but at the truth which has come home to his own heart and how good the vision is and the pattern. It may be but an outline and a cry of "this one thing I do," it will grow on us if we are faithful to that, as gardens grow from the crocus to the beauty and sweetness of May and June. Grow as those wonderful old places have grown I love to look at when I go back to the old home. There was first a strong tower of defence with a well away down in the foundations. Then a hall with living rooms and a nursery on the sunny side, then a chapel and a library and gallery and a bower set about with gardens, but the old tower still stands in the centre, and the well flows as ever down in its heart. So the first call on us comes in some such simple way for a citadel and a well and then grace for grace. One of the men I reverence most set out since I remember to make as good a broad-axe as could be made by hands, and in the glow of it (for he made the axe), he saw the picture of a home and a house-mother and a little "pulpit of wood," where he would preach Sundays, and a little library, where he would work at his books when his day's work was done. We used to stand side by side thirty-three years ago and tell our visions and get out our patterns, very simple, but they were real. He is making broad-axes still, as good as can be made, and lives but an hour from us, and I went to see him one day and it has all come true, through much frustration, but better in many ways than when he saw the vision in the glowing fires. The citadel in the centre with its well, and then the sweet grace and beauty of a workingman's home, on which he does not owe a dollar. It may be that the vision calls for a broad-axe, we must make it; a little song like the Psalm of Life, we must sing it; a little book, we must write it; a picture, we must paint it. The vision and pattern is always half the battle, and even when it seems as if the thing we try to do by this high direction never would be done so that it should answer to the fair ideal, we must not be troubled overmuch but keep right on,—we must do our best as he did who died not having received the promise, but seeing it afar off,—and leave the rest to God. Yes, and if some fair visions seem to have vanished into a mist and some patterns turned to dust so that we are ready to say, "I shall go down to the grave mourning," we must not say that, or count our life greatly a failure, or the world a poor-house or a prison, we were glad for once as a palace. It is the same world in which we were so light of heart so many years ago, no worse, but a great deal better every way, and sure to grow better as we stand by the vision and work to its fair lines. I have scars on me I shall carry to my grave. I got them when I was a boy and was caught in the machinery of a great factory. It was good machinery and was doing good work, but the bone is apt to ache, still, when the weather changes, and this is the trouble with us all who can look back on many years. We get hurt among these things that in their whole scope and purpose are doing God's work and are divine, and then we are never quite the same, every change in the soul's barometer sends word to the old hurt in the heart and starts the pain, and we are wiser in a way that makes us wish we were otherwise, but this does not touch the perfect order or the true intention. The world's mighty life rolls on, steady and true as ever, the whole trouble lies within. I know it is a trouble, but we must write Hope and Expectation high above this in grand, strong letters, and still wait and watch for the vision and the pattern to take the place of those that seem to be lost or are done with and fulfilled. There's rosemary yet, that's for remembrance, and rue, alas! but then there's a daisy, too, and only *some* violets withered, and let pansies, if it must be so, be for thoughts. Still, we must not conclude that they bloom to deck our graves only; they bloom about the cradles and in nursery windows, and are showered down on maids on their wedding-days and blossom forth for holy-days, and so it is with this fair flower of our human life and the vision and the pattern.

It is the truth, finally, touching your Church and mine, I trust, and all Churches worth the name, as it was with this in the old time and as it is with our life. The old simple and strong citadel with the well in its heart flowering forth into this, for which we are all so glad after the vision and the pattern, the striving of all the years since one cried, "Spring up, O well!" stern, strong battles fought for the truth and for fair human rights under the old leader, and still fought under the new. Something done always, and well done, like that he had in his mind as he brooded. To help make this city so noble by reason of the nobility of her citizens that she also shall be the joy of the whole earth, and a Church which should answer to the need of every man, and woman, and child within its blessed boundary, and the man true, helping to make a true and strong commonwealth. It is the old story in the new time, and time, if we are faithful, will but open out and make beautiful its deeper and more excellent secret. I must not tell you what this Church has been to me, and he who, for so many years, ministered at its altar; yet I cannot be quite silent, for that would be a shame. I mind, as if it were yesterday, the thatched cottage where I sat by a sea-coal fire on a winter night, reading a story and noticing a name belonging here across the sea, long before I saw those patterns. And it seemed as if this city was not quite so strange at first, because he lived here, your old minister; indeed, I could not be sure there was not some slender thread in the memory to draw me here. And I mind how I would fain have come through the earlier years and said to him, "Give me to drink of your well," only everybody said the waters were poisoned; so, when I came now and then on a Sunday, I went to Tenth and Arch. But I did come and sit down one Sunday evening,—a wild, wet evening,—and did drink at the well, and lo, it was very sweet and good. And he gave me his hand and so much more, the man whose story I had read on that winter evening so long before in Yorkshire, and courteously, as if I had been his good comrade, he asked me to preach for him on a day, with what misgiving he only knew, and the good saint who is in Heaven. I wonder if there are two left who mind that Sunday.

No, I cannot tell the story, only this Church will always seem so good to me and homelike, for his sake and theirs. It is told of the Moslem that, when he was an old man, he would fain go back to where he began, and said to one who was with him, "Will you not gather me fruit from that tree over there? I mind so well how sweet it was when I ate it long ago in my youth." And so I hope to come by your grace now and then, not to give, but to gather. It is a brave, new wall you have built all about, but the old garden and the fruit of the tree which yieldeth always, and whose very leaves have been, and are, for the healing of the nations, will grow only better, please God, through all the years to come.

A LIBERAL CHRISTIAN CHURCH*

BY REV. JOSEPH MAY

OF PHILADELPHIA

"The Truth shall make you free."—JOHN viii. 32.

"He left not Himself without witness."—ACTS xiv. 17.

"For the invisible things of Him are clearly seen, being understood by the things that are made."—ROMANS i. 20.

"God was in Christ reconciling the world unto Himself."—2 COR. v. 19.

"Not every one that saith unto me Lord, Lord, shall enter into the Kingdom of Heaven, but he that doeth the will of my Father which is in heaven."—MATT. vii. 21.

AFTER some congratulatory remarks, addressed to his congregation peculiarly, the speaker said:

What *are* we, friends, as organized and planted here? For what are we to stand and to work?

It is fitting on this occasion, and I do it with confidence and emphasis, that we assert our title as a branch of the Christian Church. This title the Unitarian body has never resigned, nor ceased to value. Through nearly a century of existence our own individual organization has always affectionately maintained it. Historically, Unitarianism was by no means a growth out-

---

* Sermon preached at the first regular service in the new Church of the First Society of Philadelphia, February 14, 1886, by the pastor.

side the Christian Church, nor a secession from it, in any country. Notably in our own it was a development within the Church, maintaining a strict continuity with preceding generations of the Church, and in New England, including a large proportion of its ablest clergy and most influential congregations. In our own present new life and hope we again declare ourselves a Christian Church.

And we do this not merely—not even chiefly—for our own sake, to vindicate a cherished birthright and heritage, but still more in loyalty to Christianity itself, as a protest against influences which have long wrought within the Church—against tendencies natural and persistent, but perverted and unhealthy—to make Christianity, to make religion, a thing of doctrine and belief, and not a thing of faith and life. We do it in loyalty to the truth, because we believe that erroneous and unchristian interpretation has been given in the Church to fundamental religious conceptions,—to conceptions of Providence, Faith, Prayer, Salvation, Duty, Destiny. We do it in loyalty to our fellow-men everywhere, so many of whom have been injuriously excluded from the pale of the Church and weaned from religion, through the perhaps sincere, but perverted, understanding of its constitution and of its gospel which has been imposed upon it.

The three most peculiar and characteristic assertions of the Unitarian Church have been these:

First—The right and duty of individual intellectual freedom.

Second—The unity, that is, the simplicity of the Godhead.

Third—That salvation and acceptance with God consist in character and life, not in belief.

Let me, on this epochal occasion, glance, compendiously, at these assertions.

First—Mental Freedom.

We assert, as the primary, inalienable and most important right of every human soul that it should pursue the attainment of truth uncoerced and untrammelled. To attain truth is the end and aim of human existence, and it is clear beyond question that two conditions are constitutionally essential to the work, the one of which is sincerity within the mind and the other freedom without. Genuine perception of truth is like the perception of natural objects,—it is individual and spontaneous. One may be *helped* to it, but he can no more be *forced* to perceive truth than he can be forced to see or hear with his physical organs. Either is impossible. And even when one perceives truth—if that means intellectually discerns it—the work is only begun. The intellectual perception reaches only to the form of truth. The real apprehension of it means and includes its incorporation into character, and this process is still more a vital one, which coercion may disturb, but cannot possibly effect or promote.

All that coercion, all that arbitrary authority can do is to produce conformity and a simulated belief, which, though it may even deceive the man himself, has in it no reality or quickening power. All conformity is fatal to spontaneity and therefore to genuineness. And this is the peculiar mischief which creeds do. It is not that they produce hypocrites so often as self-deceivers; souls which think they believe, when of real vital belief they have little or none.

Many a mind about us, by the rigid denial to it, from earliest days, of all mental freedom, has been wholly debarred from the real attainment of truth. Its whole relation to truth has been made mechanical, not vital. It is an automaton, not a living organism. It has never really looked at the truth with its own eyes. For that vision it has always had substituted the statements of others. So the truth has never really reached it, to touch and vivify it.

No matter, my friends, what conclusions free research and reflection lead a man to, those conclusions are better *for him* than any imposed on his mind by authority. False in form, they still have the spirit of truth in them. So they are steps in a mental process which, if kept free, kept sincere, kept active, will at length lead him to the truth. "When He, the Spirit of Truth is come," said Jesus, "He shall guide you into all truth." Inspiration, guidance, every soul needs; coercion damages whatever vital being it touches. Even the coercion of one's own past conclusions too rigidly adhered to, may be injurious to a soul. Only by keeping itself alive, and so forever free, can it be safe and feel sure that it is in the path of truth.

And this we must carefully keep in mind as we advance to another point.

The object of seeking truth being to attain it, it would be sad indeed if in nothing we could feel that we *had* attained it. We *have* to feel so; in many particulars life can only proceed on the basis of a confidence that we have attained truth. In so feeling, we recognize our own limitations; we remember that we are to progress; but for the time in which we are, we habitually repose in the conviction of certain truths of fact, or truths of principle.

So neither the vindication of our own, nor of each other's mental freedom limits the franchise, or the duty, of declaring what we come to accept as truth. To declare it, when attained, is as much a duty as to seek it is. To bear witness to truth, in the strength of our own conviction, is not, remember, to impose an opinion on another. It is only to offer it to him,—and this is a part of our mutual and highest service. Throughout life we thus help each other, and in all inquiry the sincere opinions of other careful inquirers are a most important element in our particular researches.

To declare truth, then, is a right and duty. And what is a right and duty for an individual may be the right and duty of a collection of individuals.

With whatever precaution is needful as to method we may unite to declare our faith in whatever truth has revealed itself to our minds and hearts.

Now the Church is but such a union of consenting minds. It is an outward, visible, and therefore finite, limited organization of men, which as its aim is, on the one hand, to attain truth, so, on the other, has the function to discharge of declaring truth. It stands as a witness to certain great truths. Our Unitarian warfare against creeds has not been a denial of the right of men to *issue statements* of their own beliefs; it has been a protest against the claim of any body of men, of the whole Church, of the whole race, to *impose the acceptance* of these on an individual mind under penalty of any human right or hope whatever. The danger of even statements of belief we have seen and felt. We have found that in the *details* of opinion it is next to impossible to frame statements which shall accurately reflect the sincere convictions of many consenting individuals. We have found, too, as a practical matter, that they are of very little utility. Our own congregations are as coherent, as active and as zealous, having no creeds, as those of the churches which have elaborate creeds. And we know how gladly some of these would get rid of their creeds if they could only agree upon a way to do so.

I do not believe the real integrity of the Church would be impaired a whit if she would abandon her creeds and the whole policy and method of intellectual coercion. Nay, her witness to her truths would be immensely strengthened; her whole spiritual life would be enhanced and freshened, if she would consent to stand *freely* for what she holds true, and depend—as the Unitarian Church depends—on spiritual sympathy alone as a bond of union. Let those who should love her stay; let those who ceased to trust her go; if she have truth, true souls will stay; nay, from every quarter under heaven they will flock to her through the sacred magnetism of common conviction and aspiration. To this condition I rejoice to believe the whole Church is actually tending. Heaven hasten the day! that the whole Church may experience—may experience it a hundredfold!—the quickening, warming influence which our own branch of it has enjoyed since it came fully to the position of intellectual freedom, and a union in the spirit.

But with or without her creeds, the Church as a whole would stand, as she stands, witness to certain great facts or truths. In these broadest convictions there is a unity of consent in all branches of the Church, Catholic, Protestant, Unitarian, Trinitarian, Orthodox, and Heterodox. And it is this voluntary, spontaneous *unity of conviction* that is the real strength and cement of the Church as a whole.

This is what she stands for, fundamentally and compendiously: for the great fact that *God has made Himself known to the human race.* The Church has grown up naturally (and so on this point is a living witness to it), out of the confidence of men that, as in every nation God leaves Himself not without witness, so through that centuries-long development of the Hebrew religious consciousness—through that singular reawakening of the religious consciousness of the European races which ensued on the life and preaching of Jesus and his apostles, through the twenty centuries of her own life—a real knowledge of God, a valid knowledge, has been coming into men's hearts. How this knowledge has come has been the cause of unending and perhaps futile dispute: but that it is valid knowledge, the Church stands to bear witness of her confidence as against the agnostic, who says that man cannot know God; or the ethicist, who says that it is not important whether man knows Him or not; or the atheist, who says there is no God to know.

I do not discuss to-day how this knowledge comes to man's heart; but I also, as a Unitarian, assert its validity. The mode by which it comes is usually called "revelation;" and whatever erroneous interpretations there may have been of the *process* of revelation, the *fact* of it, the *fact* that God has made Himself known to men, appears to me as indisputable as the fact that yonder sunlight pours into our windows. I am incapable of entering into the rational condition of the man who treats the history of religion as illusory; who can bring himself to suppose that all that *sense of Deity* which has characterized our race more profoundly than almost any other perception has been a delusion. Nor can I look upon the facts of our own religious history—tracing it up through all Christian ages to its source in the earliest stirrings of the emotion in our religious progenitors, the great Hebrew race—and comprehend how an intelligent person can doubt that a genuine and valid knowledge of spiritual facts and truths has been steadily coming into men's minds. The crudities, the errors of each period, the hypocrisies and offences of many periods, no more blot out the essential fact than the mists of morning or the clouds of dust from the highway blot out the sun. The world over, the *sense* of God has been, so far, a valid *knowledge* of God. God revealed Himself to the brutish hearts of men whose only conception of Him was the mystery in a crooked root or a hideous block of stone; He revealed Himself to them when they looked up and saw Him in the sun and stars, as the best conception they could then form; He revealed Himself to the Hebrews when their best thought of Him was as a tribal King, who went to battle with them, as Castor and Pollux entered into the strifes of Greeks and Romans. In every case the *form* of the conception of Deity is not the essential thing; it is temporary; it belongs to the age and the degree of men's development; the *fact of the apprehension of God* is the main thing, and the Church says, and I say, the fact is *real;* it is *not* illusory.

And you say this, when you build this house for the worship of God. Its walls and arches rise as the visible witness to the fact that *God has made Himself known to men.*

But we call this church a Christian Church,—as the prevalent religion of the Western world calls itself Christian. All that I have thus far said is as true of one nation or race as another. "God has not left Himself without witness" among any of His peoples. But when we say "Christian" we imply a peculiarity. What is this?

I have insisted on the validity of that knowledge of God which, for example, came to the Hebrew people; to Jacob, when he called his resting-place "Beth-el," "God's house;" to David, when he declared "blessed be Jehovah, my God, who teacheth my hands to war—my fingers to fight"—and when he said, "Jehovah is my Shepherd, I shall not want;" to Isaiah, when he said, "The everlasting God, Jehovah, the Creator of the ends of the earth, fainteth not, neither is weary; there is no searching of His understanding. He giveth power to the faint, and to them that have no might He increaseth strength;" to the whole Hebrew people when again and again they built up their temple and worshipped God as best they understood Him.

Now, there is one instance of this kind so remarkable, so transcendently vivid, beautiful, inspiring, and instructive to others, that, as a matter of historical fact, it has made an unexampled impression on the feelings and faith of men. More and more clear and pure had the knowledge of God been coming to be among his people, and for a century or two it had, in their best minds, become very spiritual and beautiful.

But—through what consenting circumstances we can never now tell—to *this* imperial soul such a revelation of God came as men have seen equal tokens of in no other. Jesus seemed to know God as a man his friend, as the child its father; and his life so illustrated, his lips so exquisitely formulated and conveyed this knowledge, that he has become, by perfectly natural causes, the leader of men in the knowledge of God. As through the phenomena of the external universe God reveals some attributes of His being to men's minds, so through the experiences of a human soul, through the life which His presence with it enkindles, He especially may reveal Himself to other hearts. What you cannot quite feel by yourself, you may perceive another man feeling. This feeling often helps yours. His faith may strengthen your faith. It is thus that in all departments of life the *leaders* of men are elected to their leadership. Men feel truth in them which they cannot feel without them, or not so well. So they trust them and follow them, *seeing through them* what they can but imperfectly see apart from them.

Now, in a manner, as I say, unexampled, this has been true in the case of Jesus. The presence of God in his soul has been practically and really a revelation to the souls of myriads of brother-men. Not only did his exquisite character furnish them new ideas of moral excellence, which they might ascribe to Deity, but *the oneness of his soul with God brought God nearer to them.* As he was deeply at one with God, God was richly present in him, and in this reflection, through this lens, they were able to discern God, as they could not unaided.

This is the substance of what has been called the revelation by Christ. The term Christ means the "anointed one." As thus at one with God, anointed by His spirit, Jesus was called by this term. It designates the spiritual man in him, in its union with God. And this spiritual manhood, united with God, through faith, love, righteousness, became, as a matter of fact, the vehicle of the knowledge of God to half a world. "*God was in Christ reconciling the world unto Himself.*"

To this *peculiar* fact, then, secondly, the Church stands as a witness. The Church grew up in virtue of its recognition of the knowledge which came to men through the knowledge of God and union with God to which Jesus attained, and which made him the Christ. It is a monument to the validity of this knowledge. Say, rather, it is the fruitful vine which from that seed grew up, branched into a hundred lands, and, still vital and growing, lives and grows in virtue of that knowledge as its sap.

Certainly, this knowledge has not been sufficient to keep men from a thousand manifest and often terrible errors; from many and many a sin; from many a present doubt. I say only that it has been *real, valid* knowledge. Its interpretations have been various and discordant. Against the most prominent of them, which has shaped and colored the whole Church, we Unitarians in particular have steadily protested, for we hold that it has hidden, perverted, despiritualized the real truth. But this remains, that there was, and the Church is called the

Christian Church, and we call ours a Christian Church, because we see that there was a new, deeper knowledge of God spread abroad through the world from the Christ life, the Christ faith of Jesus, and we accept this knowledge as valid. We accept the leadership of Jesus because we feel that in this he had the Truth in him; and so he becomes to us a *way;* becomes to us *life.* We surrender no freedom; we abandon no mental right or obligation; but we through conviction accept our place in that stream of spiritual knowledge which, flowing eternally from God, flowing through the spiritual experience of Jesus' own race, was so enlarged, reinforced, illuminated by that which flowed into and again flowed out from the heart of Jesus.

In the acceptance of these broad truths the Unitarian is at one with all the other branches of the Christian Church. Wherein she is peculiar has been implied. Accompanying the Christian movement, a great body of doctrines; of particular beliefs; of interpretations of great fundamental truths have been evolved. Of these we, individually, accept some and reject some. But, broadly, we do not admit or preach that the acceptance of *any* doctrine—even of the great foundation truths—except through free and genuine conviction, can be beneficial to any soul, or can be an acceptable offering to the God of truth. And we do not consider that the honest rejection of any doctrine, even of the actual truth, can expose a soul to the Divine censure or to any penalties, except the natural ones which must needs ensue from even sincerely preferring error to truth, and which, wherever there is freedom, tend to self-correction. We hold the acceptance or rejection of ideas, offered as truth, to be a strictly individual matter, in which it is the right and duty of the individual to be left perfectly free. To offer one's thought, to state it however earnestly, is one thing; to enforce its acceptance by any sort of penalty or threat is another. The first is right and a duty; the second is wrong and an offence.

Thus asserting the mental freedom of the individual while recognizing and accepting that revelation of Divine Truth which comes to us so richly through Jesus, we are properly called, and call ourselves, "*liberal Christians.*"

Let us, in this ninetieth year of the existence of our Church, comparing the spirit of the days when it was founded with that of the present time, rejoice that—while so much remains to be done and gained—there is such a wide extension of the spirit of liberality, which is the true spirit of Christianity, throughout all the Christian community.

But I said that the first characteristic assertion of our Church being the moral principle of spiritual freedom, the second has been the theological principle,—the unity of the Godhead. So has thought advanced and the spirit of the times changed, you would take a languid interest in a metaphysical discussion such as kept the churches of New England in a ferment seventy or eighty years ago. I do not remember that I ever devoted a sermon to a discussion of the doctrine of the Trinity. But, on an occasion like this, there is reason for a brief consideration of a point which, not very fortunately, has given us our denominational name.

Our fathers, in that great debate of the early decades of this century, maintained that the doctrine of the

Trinity was, first, scripturally unfounded, second, metaphysically absurd. I believe that they were right on both points. There is nothing approaching an adequate foundation for the doctrine in the Scriptures. A few texts may be so construed as to imply it, but this only by a degree of violence. If it had been true to the Hebrew consciousness or to that of the first generations of Christians, it would, on the other hand, have *permeated* their literature, as it does that of Orthodox Christians at the present day. The one seemingly clear statement of it (in 1 John v. 7) has always been admitted by fair scholars to be an interpolation and has been expunged from the new version.

On the other hand the *genesis* of the doctrine is perfectly well known. It grew up slowly in the Church, and did not reach a complete and defined statement till even A.D. 381, although its effective victory was won by Athanasius in the Council of Nicæa in 325.

It was a product of that speculative method which, under the forms of Gnosticism and Neo-Platonism, so called, attempted to account for the origin of the universe, to fathom the mysteries of the Divine Being, and especially to bridge the gulf between Deity and Humanity. A persistent result of this speculative effort was that conception of an intermediate agent in creation and Providence called the "Wisdom" or the "Word" of God—the "Logos"—referred to in the opening chapter of St. John's Gospel; and with this conception Jesus, as the Christ, came to be identified, and so, at length, identified with Deity by a process which it is perfectly easy to trace and to account for.

It is for me now only to say, as of the scriptural

grounds for the doctrine of the Trinity, so of the speculative. They are equally inadequate and fanciful. The Christly oneness of Jesus with God was not a confusion of personalities,—which it is anthropomorphic, absurd, and I hold it profane, to postulate,—but a spiritual oneness such as he called on all men to enter into.

Nevertheless, my friends, the yearning and the effort, out of which that great doctrine grew, are essential in humanity and affectingly characteristic of it. The great struggle at Nicæa was really to prevent a conception fastening itself on the Church which should place Deity inaccessibly away from humanity. The great need of the human heart is to feel God *near*. The great truth of religion is that He *is* near, ready to be at one with every human soul. The doctrine of the Trinity meets this want crudely and states this truth in a form which is unspiritual and false. But it was, perhaps, the only attainable statement in the unspiritual, metaphysical era when it was formulated, and, founded in a great truth, it has not wholly failed of the effect of truth. The human God which it has presented to the world has been an accessible God. And through Christ, conceived to be God, myriads have reached the God who was truly in him, and has truly been seen in him. There is no thoughtful mind to-day, whatever its doctrinal beliefs, but must rejoice that the issue of the Council of Nice was what it was.

In its most modern forms of presentation, the doctrine of the Trinity offers little which it would concern any one to cavil at. It is a question, mainly, of the use of words, especially of what the word "person" means.

I have heard statements of it from preachers and professors of unquestioned orthodoxy, into which I could enter far and with deep sympathy. It is against the bald substitution of Christ for the Father, by which Deity, in His most august and lovely attributes, is almost banished from the thought and faith and love of men, that we have especially to protest. The God whom Jesus worshipped is almost unknown in many a Christian church. And reduced to the mere proportions of a man, Deity is deprived of the majesty which belongs to God and makes Him a fitting object of worship. Here is a great moral and spiritual *loss*, to repair which should be our unceasing effort, and which makes our title, "Unitarian," still one of profound significance to society.

But our protest against the orthodoxy of our time lays its emphasis even more upon another point, the consideration of which leads me naturally to the third assertion of which I spoke at the outset of these remarks as essentially characteristic of our movement: that is, our Unitarian affirmation that *Salvation consists in character and not in belief.*

We protest explicitly and emphatically against the interpretation which has been and is given to that profound idea of atonement with God, and which too widely prevails in the orthodox Churches. I know of no caprice of language so deplorable as that which, through a mere change in pronunciation, has from the word "at-one-ment" produced the word "atonement." But even this is one of the unfortunate fruits of that conception which has so long held its place in the Church that the work of Christ is in reconciling God to men, not in leading men to God. The doctrine of the atonement has undergone constant and radical modifications from generation to generation. Its form has totally altered more than once. Its spirit is at the present time profoundly ameliorated. But even as now preached, it is generally calculated to pervert the moral sense and to undermine moral character.

A debilitating reliance upon Christ to do for men what they ought to do for themselves is still a characteristic outcome of the presentation of this doctrine.

No such conception or tendency has any support in the thought of Jesus, or in the writings of Paul. It is a radical perversion of the true Christianity, historically inevitable, no doubt, but from which it is the chief hope of the Church that it is slowly recovering. Meantime, then, our office is by no means yet discharged, if holding up the true view; that of individual human responsibility; of salvation as the perfection of character; of at-one-ment with God as the harmonizing of our wills, and thoughts, and desires, and aims with His, in lives practically conformed to these monitions of the Holy Spirit, whose voice is conscience and the aim of which is ideal perfection. To all this, right belief is of immense importance; and the study of the abstract truth of God must continue a responsibility of the highest consequence. But the at-one-ment of each private soul with God resides in the will; and he whose will is radically and unreservedly united with God's, can neither stray far from God's ways, nor fail at length of His truth. "He that is willing to do the will of my Father," said Jesus, "shall know of the doctrine."

And so now, dear friends, I hesitate not on this

epochal occasion to renew the declaration of our fathers in Unitarianism that the practical union of the wills of men with God's, manifested in good lives, is the last and only sufficient token of true religion in them and the one final acceptable offering to God. The moral conformity of life and conduct to the highest standard of conscience is the only sufficient test of a man's personal religion. "He who *doeth the will* of God is accepted with Him." *Righteousness* is the sure and necessary form of every life in which religion is really established as its central principle. That any belief whatever can be a substitute for moral excellence as a ground of acceptance with God, as a token of discipleship to Jesus (whose life was spent in doing good), or as a proof to other men of one's religiousness, is so monstrous and wicked and anti-Christian a proposition, that, had it not actually been preached and accepted in the Church, it would be utterly incredible that any one should frame it. To God, who is truth, it must be utterly profane and abhorrent; of the teachings of Jesus it is a flagrant and contemptuous denial; of the doctrine of faith formulated by St. Paul, and so profoundly true, it is a shallow and often an impudent travesty. St. John, most spiritual of the New Testament writers, says,—and how could words be plainer or more emphatic?—"Ye know that Christ was manifested to *take away sins*" (not even "sin," in the abstract, but "sins," our actual wrongs and vices), . . . "whosoever abideth in him *sinneth not;* whosoever sinneth hath not seen him, neither knoweth him. My little children, let no man lead you astray; *he that doeth righteousness is righteous* even as he is righteous; he that *doeth sin* is of the devil." "To this end was the Son of

God manifested that he might *destroy the works of the devil.* Whosoever is begotten of God doeth no sin." . . . "*Whosoever doeth not righteousness is not of God,* neither he that loveth not his brother."

Let no man say that the ethical emphasis of Unitarianism, which has been always its most marked and characteristic trait, has not warrant of Scripture,—when such a passage as that is from the very pen, as usually supposed, of the beloved disciple of him, whose first word to the world was "repent," every one of whose beatitudes was pronounced on ethical worthiness, and who summed up all his requirements in the demand that men should perfect themselves,—even making the perfection of Deity their standard!

To this witness of our fathers, my friends, let us be true in the future, as I humbly hope we have not been altogether wanting in the past. To the practical moral and humane service of society let us distinctly consecrate our fresh new temple. Let its doors open as by instinct to every cause which promises to benefit mankind. May many a word be spoken from this platform which shall encourage right, expose evil, touch hearts with love and pity and arouse them to faithful duty. The proudest record of our history as a society is the fidelity of my beloved predecessor to the rights of man, cruelly denied in his day and vindicated only through years of cloud and storm and blood and fire. I pray to God that in spirit, in fidelity, and in freedom the standard of its pulpit may, by God's grace, never be less high or less manfully maintained, cost what it may. Should Mammon and Fashion ever enter here and drive out Truth and Love and Service, may these walls crumble and hide themselves in congenial dust and shame!

Here, then, dear friends, almost within the last decade of our century of life as an organization, with precious traditions and tender memories as the legacy of our past, and in fulness of present joy and hope, we stand to do the work which God shall call us to!

Shall we do it faithfully or shall we fail? What resolutions can we frame? What new incentives can I offer that shall keep us in the right way, that shall make our hearts tender and unworldly, loving towards each other and towards the God who has so richly blessed us in every spiritual and every earthly way? As I think of our abundant homes; as I think of our beautiful new religious home; as I think of the blessings of education, emancipation of mind and confidence towards God which have been vouchsafed us; as I think of the traditions of our own movement, and of our own Church, in which there is so much to guide and inspire us; above all, as I think that God *is*, is ever with us, is all-loving, all-patient, seeking ever to bring us to Himself, and as I think of that holy personality through whom He has been so richly manifested to us, who is our brother, and whom it is our privilege, if we will, to make our friend,—as I think of all these things, we seem to be, indeed, "a peculiar people," who cannot exact from ourselves too much of service in God's cause of bringing all men to holiness, purity, peace and union with Him. I wonder if we all feel as deeply, as we should, His goodness and what we owe to Him? I wonder if our hearts are tender and grateful enough to-day? If we are meaning, or striving to mean, to do, severally and together, all that our privileges and our abilities call us to do? "Freely we have received; freely let us give." *May God make us faithful!*

One cannot enter here to-day and not wonder a little, with venial curiosity, what shall be the fortunes of this church, now standing, new and fresh, in the bright morning light! We have built it—but not for ourselves. Our occupancy may not be for very long. Few, even of these youngest, shall follow it through the half-century or so, which is all such a building is apt to see. New faces, new voices, shall be here. Joy shall come to most of us. The bride and her husband shall stand before this altar. Grief shall come to all; the dead shall lie here. The deeper sorrow of sin, the anguish of remorse, the yearning of penitence, may come in hither, hidden in men's bosoms. Anxiety and doubt shall come in to gain rest and peace. May aspiration come, and true prayer rise from many, many hearts!

We can forecast nothing! Blessed be God that He is over us and with us,—"over all, and through all, and in all." He will care for us and for our successors; and they and we shall be happy and safe if all are but true. God make us true! God soften our hearts! May He take this new house of ours for His abiding-place, sanctify all its associations, quicken its every particle with inspiration, and make it for every soul who shall enter here truly a gate of heaven! Amen.

THE END.

www.ingramcontent.com/pod-product-compliance
Lightning Source LLC
Chambersburg PA
CBHW031813220426
43662CB00007B/633